I0113776

RENEWING YOUR MIND

Perspectives of a Christian Hypnotist

Anthony M. Davis, BCH, CTACC

Copyright © 2018 Anthony M. Davis
Center for Personal Leadership and Development
www.leadership-matters.org

All rights reserved.

No part of this book may be used or reproduced in any manner without written permission of the author, except for brief quotations used in reviews and critiques.

Contact for Use Permissions:
info@leadership-matters.org

This book is not intended as a substitute for the medical or mental health advice of licensed physicians or mental health practitioners. The reader should regularly consult a physician in matters relating to his/her health and particularly with respect to any symptoms that may require diagnosis or medical attention.

Book Antiqua & Cambria fonts used with permission from Microsoft.
Cover Photo: From Pixabay.com under Creative Commons CC0.

Printed in the United States of America.

ISBN-13: 978-1-732318601

Large Print Edition 2018

A Path to Follow

"Do not conform to the pattern of this world, but be transformed by the renewing of your mind. Then you will be able to test and approve what God's will is — his good, pleasing and perfect will."

~ Romans 12:2

Acknowledgment

Nothing in this text can be written without giving credit to God who makes all things possible.

In spite of myself, God helped me find a path I probably would not have chosen on my own. My vision for the future was clouded by my own internal focus. Once I realized that God is, in fact, the one that gave me life with an eternal hope, it only made sense to acknowledge my sin and yield to His plan. Even then my own impatience and frustrations provided no value other than a slow lesson over time that He knows what is best.

Each time I hesitated to continue writing this book, He brought new experiences and interactions to me that each provided substance to bring it to completion.

Contents

PART 3
PUTTING IT TO ACTION

PART 1

FINDING
&
DEFINING
HYPNOSIS

1

Introduction

It's hard to quantify the number of people in the world that understand hypnosis and those who don't. Hollywood, stage performances and spectacular news stories by those that don't understand this modality have left people confused. It's easier to believe the negative and typically, that's what people remember. Coming from an investigative background has taught me that uncovering truths takes effort. With a society that shows a tendency to make decisions based on social network posts or other people's opinions, the truth can easily become elusive.

Some have condemned me exhibiting negative behavior and chose to be at odds with hypnosis because of a perceived notion that it is dangerous or un-Christian. Frankly, it's not my intent to convince anyone to believe that hypnosis is real or not.

As a Christian hypnotist, I share my experiences based on what I have seen with my own eyes with client after client after client. It's my hope to offer information and details of experiences to make your own intelligent decisions. I'm not responsible for your beliefs - you are.

I believe the introduction of a book like this should be more than an overview of the text ahead; it should also provide the context of the author writing the words. Without knowing the person, you'll never fully understand the experiences and feelings behind the perspectives shared in the book.

My background includes growing up in an abusive and violent environment. It becomes a life-long challenge to not let those years define who a person is and their perception of things around them. All that said, I believe we should avoid becoming a person that waves the, "*I'm a victim*" flag. Ironically, a large percentage of my clients arrive carrying some of the same burdens (or worse). This is precisely an area where hypnosis is helpful.

Living in the past never moves a person forward. Yet, when there were struggles, hurts or unhealthy environments behind us, it's important to remain cognizant of where we came from so each day ahead becomes a blessing.

Once on my own, I floated around awhile looking for something that would stick and look like a viable career path. It wasn't until I found God, everything began to change. He was there all along; I just wasn't looking for Him.

Having served in two military services and law enforcement, I learned a lot about people. I also learned a lot about myself. I believe those experiences were in some way a preparation for my work later to help people through my professional coaching and hypnosis sessions.

To be clear, I am not some spiritual warrior. I'm fully capable of experiencing hurts, fears, worries, and frustrations – that comes with being human. Only now, I know how to overcome those challenges I once faced. Throughout this book, you'll see both the high and low points as I describe the path with hypnosis.

Some will read these pages and say I'm *"Too Christian"*. That's okay. My goal is to be real so that you will gain an understanding of the issue of Christianity and Hypnosis. When you recognize the value of a safe and natural process, you will then have options to overcome your own challenges.

As the reader, I don't know where your faith walk is. I do believe that nothing happens by accident and you have this book in your life at this time for a reason, perhaps for your own self-assessment.

It's my hope that you will view this text objectively and question how it could be a help to your own life. At the end of the day, no one can make you think a thought without your permission.

I also understand that this topic may push some buttons for people. There are some in the church that may determine to stick with the *"Hypnosis is bad"* belief.

Making a choice not to consider alternatives is easier, particularly with a topic that seems like an intangible thing. It's not something we can hold in our hands.

The science of the brain yields fascinating results with Electroencephalogram (EEG) and Functional Magnetic Resonance Imaging (fMRI). Such testing shows that brain wave function changes when given varying stimuli during hypnosis.[1] It's my belief that some non-science individuals won't dig that deep to research hypnosis. It's easier for a person to assume something is bad based on what they may have heard over the years.

There are many non-Christian hypnosis practitioners operating worldwide that are highly proficient, invest their time and efforts into their client's best. Through their skill and experience, many lives are changing in positive ways. Yet, as this book will describe, there are areas where we will disagree.

My disagreement with those particular areas does not indicate these practitioners are bad. Quite the contrary. Many of these professionals are people I care for and respect. It's my hope we can share the same professional courtesy. Time will tell how that works out.

As a society, we have moved into a place where logical or moral disagreement turns into personal attacks. The party claiming offense then justifies their behavior. Such behavior is not a hypnosis problem - it's a sin problem.

To be clear, it's important that you understand my optic. My view is that of a Christian hypnotist that has seen lives change through this modality. Yet, I am a Christian before I am a Hypnotist. As you'll see in the pages ahead, there are areas I go, and places I won't because my faith comes first. The pages ahead explain why.

2

Discovering Hypnosis

If someone were to tell me I would be a hypnotist, I would have thought them to be crazy, or at least in need of a drug test. I've spent a lifetime in two military services amidst seemingly endless cycles of operations. As I later transitioned to serve in law enforcement and other government-related positions, I pursued facts or the indicators of them.

I didn't fully understand hypnosis so it was easier to disbelieve it was anything more than stage entertainment or over-dramatized mind control exhibited in old black and white movies.

In my younger years as a 17-year old sailor in the Navy, I participated in a stage hypnosis show. I was aware of most things that happened and while it all seemed pretty silly, I blamed it on a couple of beers beforehand and my wanting to have fun. I never gave it another thought.

Yet decades later I was working in an unhealthy environment with suicides and co-workers overloaded with management-induced stressors.

In my earlier years, I grew up in a violent and abusive environment. Over time, a person becomes skilled at internalizing their feelings. When the internal stressors began to impact my health, I knew I needed to take action and find healthy ways to stay strong and move forward. The thought of seeking hypnosis to resolve my *"issues and baggage"* wasn't even a consideration. Yet, carrying unnecessary baggage is like putting a piece of clay in your pocket each time an emotional trigger comes along.

Rather than take action, we pick up another piece of clay. Over time, our pockets get full and we move up to a backpack to carry around more worries, fears, anger and negative perceptions of ourselves.

We eventually get a wagon to carry all of our backpacks everywhere we go. We become defined by the negative and yet familiar garbage in our wagon. The goodness within us and the hopes and dreams we once had as a child fades away into obscurity.

Our baggage becomes so familiar to us that we cling to it rather than try to free ourselves from the weight. Our burdens become a familiar foe that we often battle. We justify their existence with excuses like, *"That's just who I am"*.

Often times we allow ourselves to believe the lie that enjoying a good, healthy and loving relationship, or successful life is for someone else – not us. That's where I found myself. I was striving for success while not believing I was capable of actually achieving it.

I felt as though I was on a never-ending treadmill of busyness and needed to find healthy solutions to neutralize the stress or turn it into something positive that challenged me. As I sought to change, I reconnected with a woman I knew 30-years earlier.

Back then she was a young model and radio broadcaster and I was a freelance photographer shooting her portfolio. Now three decades later, she is a successful hypnotist.

Thinking back, I remember her telling me about the book, *"The Power of Positive Thinking"* by Norman Vincent Peale.[2] Even then, that book was planting seeds in her life and making a difference. As she talked about the book, I didn't see any connection to it that fit my life at the time. She had the Christian faith – I didn't.

Now decades later, she was telling me about her hypnosis business and how she got there. She inquired about my career path and I told her about my military service, law enforcement and touched upon another position causing me stress. As intuitive as she is, it didn't take much for her to surmise that the joy I once had for the job was sucked out of my life like so many others around me.

As I watched a toxic environment forming, I began to feel an uncomfortable sense of stress pulling away from my ability to perform well in my job. As an aside, this workplace environment is not isolated to where I was working. I regularly see new clients on the receiving end of the misbehavior from bad managers.

This is the primary reason why I restructured my business from Healing Hypnosis to the Center for Personal Leadership and Development. My intent is to offer professional Coaching and Hypnosis resources allowing people to move forward and live a fruitful life.

Those locked in by personal circumstances or the real estate market hung in there. I knew I needed to find positive internal change and the work I was doing was important. Internally, I knew I needed to find a healthy balance to continue providing my best to the organization.

Yet the environment kept pushing me into an unhealthy place physically, emotionally and spiritually. My friend suggested hypnosis and referred me to a program called 7th PATH®,[3] a spiritually-based program that helps clear the junk out of our lives.

When she suggested hypnosis, I wasn't sure I even believed in it. I remember clear as day thinking, *"What else have you got?"* Realistically, I really didn't have much. When I first met her nearly 30-years earlier, I lacked a faith base of any kind. Now, things were different.

During the Christmas season, 28-years earlier I found the saving relationship with Christ that I needed so badly. No longer was Christ an ornament on a tree or name that we hear in Christmas carols. I came to understand that this Jesus suffered and died on a cross for me.

Truth be told, I'm still figuring this out decades later. In the same way, human relationships ebb and flow so does a personal connection with Christ until the relationship matures.

I describe this awareness because it's important to understand my mindset when becoming aware of hypnosis. A spiritually-based self-hypnosis program seemed less threatening to me at that time. Yet, I was still ignorant of hypnosis or how it would align with my faith (or not). Given her faith base, she was able to ease my concerns a bit and cautiously, I began to check this thing out. I was both hopeful and scared because I didn't know what hypnosis is, and was unsure what would happen.

At this point in my life, I was heading toward an unhealthy

place. I wasn't smoking or drinking or doing drugs. I wasn't carousing in places where I shouldn't be. I was just feeling lost. I knew something had to change and I thought, *"What have I got to lose?"*

I listened to some 7th PATH® audios I found online and in a matter of days, I noticed a new level of excitement about life. I felt lighter and my thoughts were clearer. A truth crept to the surface that I already knew: *"The world is full of knuckleheads but you don't have to let them drive you."*

That simple truth helped clarify my need to take control of my life. There are always people circling around us flinging rocks and flaming arrows in our day to day lives. Yet, we no longer need to take cover and hope for the best.

We are fully capable of responding to our environment with courage and control. Given the change I began to see within myself, I wondered about others who might be like me. How could I help them?

3

The Next Step

Still, as a Christian, I needed to know more about this hypnosis thing. I wanted to know with certainty I wasn't risking my faith or engaging in some voodoo or other cult-like activity. I know this may sound absurd but there are many people today who need help that have the same fears, unknowing what hypnosis is or is not. To allay my concerns, I opted to follow scriptural advice that tells us to, "*Study to show yourself approved*".[4] At this juncture, I enrolled in a 50-hour foundation course to learn the basic facts. It was important to know I wasn't crossing some line that God may have drawn in the sand.

The course wasn't intended to make me a hypnotist by any means. The lessons and practical exercises gave me a working description of hypnosis from a mind and body perspective and it clarified many of my misperceptions. Up until this course, I was doing self-hypnosis.

After completing the foundation course, I was hypnotizing other people. It's a unique, nervous and exciting experience when you help someone else reach a hypnotic state for the first time.

Hollywood and stage hypnotists make it easy to become confused about hypnosis. Aside from the entertainment value of a hypnosis stage show, my only interest was to help people overcome challenges using this natural state.

Once I learned the effective boundary lines for working with the mind and body, I realized I now had the potential to make positive, life-giving changes in people's lives.

In any profession, I believe it's important to receive quality training, be part of a professional organization, and have safe and legal ground rules such as a Code of Ethics.

I wish I could tell you that there are not hypnotists out there that took a short course, watched a few videos or read a book and went into business. There are areas that hypnotists should not go without a medical referral. Yet, some clearly advertise those areas that blur the lines of a legal scope of practice. I'll discuss this further in a later chapter.

During my initial search for a quality certification program, I found some that appeared as a bunch of used car salesmen wearing hypnosis trainer hats. They would be anything I wanted to them to be as long as I invested in their training program.

Now I don't bring up these points to disparage hypnosis trainers. There are some very good ones I know that I would refer to. My point is whether you are looking for a hypnotist, dentist, plumber or a mechanic; the requirement for due diligence is on you. Look for training, certifications, and experience.

My search was narrowed down to a trainer associated with the National Guild of Hypnotists (NGH).[5] The NGH is the oldest and largest professional Hypnotism organization in the world. Today, at the time of this writing, the organization is nearing 19,000 members from around the globe.

Over decades of development, their training program created a proficiency standard so that an NGH Hypnotist will have the requisite knowledge, skills, and abilities to practice successfully. Each year they host well over 100 training courses, require ongoing Continuing Education Units (CEU) and they operate within an approved Code of Ethics.

Years ago in an earlier career as a federal investigator, I had cases where members of the public were injured or killed by industries failing to incorporate designated standards of care within their profession. Granted, that may seem like a drastic comparison to hypnosis. Yet, here's my point: Industries that care enough to define professional standards tend to be successful.

Given the NGH focus of ongoing training, professional standards, and a viable Code of Ethics, all those are important to me. These criteria along with a professional focus led me to a reputable clinical hypnosis program.

A week after becoming a Certified Consulting Hypnotist, I opened my practice and began seeing new clients. In those early days, I think I was more afraid of my first clients than they were of me. Yet, hypnosis is an interpersonal process; we deal with people and their lives.

We become better as practitioners by learning from each person and I quickly began to recognize familiar underlying emotional triggers in my clients.

Some of the triggers I was seeing were similar to those from my abusive past as a kid. Because of those earlier years, I had a deeply-rooted understanding of what they were feeling, and why.

My initial certification prepared me to work with direct suggestion. Depending on the issue, there is value to the basic approach. Yet, my intent was to give my clients more at a personal level. Each person is different and they need the best care, designed for them. Given the emotional triggers they carried, advanced training was necessary in order to do the deeper work.

I then enrolled in an advanced training program and became certified as an advanced-trained Five-Phase Advanced Transformational Hypnosis (5-PATH®)[6] practitioner.

With an increasing number of abuse clients, this approach can neutralize long-lasting fears, worries, anger and a host of other emotional triggers.

Having seen the incredible positive changes in lives that were once believed irreparable, anything less is like hiding the true person behind a Band-Aid.

4

What Hypnosis Is

Watch any old Bela Lugosi movie or stage performance and you'll see a person in hypnosis locked in a deep trance, appearing mentally controlled with no choice other than complete obedience. When told to say or do anything suggested of them, a person will immediately comply with, *"Yes Master"* and follow orders. This is a myth that's been propagated by the stage and screen for decades.

The reality is, during hypnosis, you are completely aware of everything that is said or done. There is no mind control by the Hypnotist because you are in control at all times. No one can make you say or do anything without your permission. You will never give up secrets that you want to hold close. If during a hypnosis session, I asked you to give me your passwords and pin numbers, you would be fully aware, in control and likely tell me to go jump in a lake.

In hypnosis, you cannot get stuck in an unbreakable trance. Throughout each day, our brain naturally transitions through various brain wave frequencies. If left unattended in hypnosis for a period of time, you might transition to a sleep stage and then wake up, or more likely, simply emerge to a normal waking state.

I sometimes jokingly tell my clients that if I had a heart attack while they are hypnotized, they would simply open their eyes and hopefully call 911. To alleviate any fear of me having a heart attack during our session, I generally tell them, *"I checked my calendar and it's not on my schedule...So, we're good".*

This lightens the mood by introducing some humor to eliminate any nervousness they may have about the upcoming session. Scripture tells us, *"A cheerful heart is a good medicine."*[7] I've found when clients smile and laugh a little, they generally reach a comfortable level of hypnosis quicker, and that helps them get rid of stress.

During normal day-to-day activities, our brainwaves operate in a Beta state. This is the normal waking state. When transitioning to a sleep stage, our minds slow down and operate in what is known as a Delta state. At other points throughout each 24-hour day, you may shift to an Alpha or Theta state. These are times when we naturally fade in and out of a light state of hypnosis.

YOU'VE ALREADY BEEN HYPNOTIZED

You may never have been to a hypnotist and yet, you have been hypnotized thousands of times in your life. At times as a child or perhaps your present life, you found yourself in a daydream. With your thoughts so transfixed on a situation or a place, the momentary daydream seemed real to you.

During these times, your imagination allows you to think in

pictures. You might have felt relaxed or experienced some other physical sensation consistent with the daydream. You were actually in a state of hypnosis.

Perhaps there were times when you read a book, watched a movie or listened to a song and you had an emotional or physical response. You might even find yourself at the point of tears. You know it is just a book, movie, a song or some other stimulus and yet, you experienced emotional feelings. Being so focused on the storyline you entered a light state of hypnosis. As a result, you became highly suggestible and experienced feelings that were coherent with your focused thoughts.

If you're like me, you might watch a little television at night. While I generally limit TV viewing to about an hour unless watching a movie, I still find myself impacted by the suggestions in front of me. Do you ever find yourself getting hungry when the food commercials come on? I do. Even though we may have had a full meal a short time earlier, we find ourselves thinking about that darn cheeseburger displayed at larger than life size on the screen.

Similar to the daydream, we are focused and the subconscious mind becomes suggestible. This is another light state of hypnosis that advertisers are very much aware of.

One of the most common ways that we naturally enter in and out of hypnosis is when we are driving. Highway hypnosis can occur when we are focused on the road ahead of us. Have you had the experience of driving and suddenly you couldn't recall the last few miles? In fact, you might have even missed the exit without knowing it. Again, this is a light state of hypnosis.

Let's look at this closer. You have just driven along the highway in a large 2,000-pound rolling missile and you don't remember the last few minutes. Why didn't you go off the road, hit another vehicle or find a tree? The answer to that question lies within your subconscious mind.

I'll explain the different parts of the mind shortly, but in this instance, just know that the subconscious mind remains fully aware and alert as a protective part of your brain. Through earlier learned experiences and muscle memory, the subconscious mind kept you in your lane and out of harm's way.

This is an important point to clarify: Hypnosis is not sleep. If you fall asleep while driving, there's a very good chance that tragedy will come if you drive off the road, find that tree, or another vehicle. In this case, the subconscious mind acts as your autopilot of sorts, keeping you in your lane.

Please note that this is not an excuse to operate a vehicle while under the influence of drugs or alcohol, to text and drive or any other form of distracted driving.

A person placing the public or themselves in harm's way, expecting their subconscious mind to take over, lacks personal responsibility. Too many people are hurt or killed by these behaviors. The subconscious mind won't act responsibly unless you are responsible.

5

The Parts of the Mind

Our mind and body are incredibly made. In the same way, a finely-tuned timepiece operates efficiently with a variety of differing components, our mind interacts with a multitude of parts collectively working in harmony with one another. The portion of your mind reading these pages is your Conscious Mind. As you progress through each page of this book, your conscious mind is making analytical judgments: *"Do I believe the author's points...or not?"*

The conscious mind is the most critical portion from a judgmental perspective, yet the least used. Even in the midst of the most detailed project or task, this portion of the mind is limited to a storage or processing capacity of only 7 to 9 bits of information at any moment in time.[8]

The conscious mind is referred to as the *"Critical Factor"*[9] because it is the most judgmental, constantly weighing a scale of belief or disbelief about each situation or environment.

The Unconscious Mind is the hidden hero, constantly operating behind the scenes.[10] We take it for granted with little thought of this multi-faceted control room. In fact, without it, we would not be thinking of anything. The unconscious mind operates on auto-pilot and controls automatic life-preserving functions, the heartbeat, respiration, blood pressure and more. In total, it controls the autonomic system that keeps us alive.

The Subconscious Mind is a true powerhouse when it comes to our thoughts and habits. This is an extremely vital part of the mind that drives our thoughts, beliefs, and behaviors. Within the subconscious mind, every memory, experience, feeling, every book you've read, every song you've heard or sung, and details of every person you've ever known are cataloged within this incredible storage bank.

Earlier I described how the conscious mind (the part you are using right now to read this) makes analytical judgments at each moment. While that part is critical in nature, the subconscious mind is literal and non-judgmental. As new data, thoughts, and experiences are registered, they are generally accepted and stored to determine future behaviors based on your thoughts and feelings.

In other words, when your thoughts and feelings are consistent with each other, your subconscious mind registers the scenario as safe and normal. If your thoughts are incongruent where you think one thing and feel another, then your subconscious mind may store that scenario as a threat.

This state creates a protection response (fight), an action to get away (flight), or force distraction to ease discomfort caused by the disagreement within yourself. The subconscious mind is protective in nature and seeks to find a sense of harmony in our lives. Yet it also reacts in unhealthy ways if discomfort is perceived. In a later chapter, we'll look at this reaction state that causes habits.

When we discuss the mind and body, we tend to separate them as two individual entities. The more I study and interact with clients, the more I'm leaning toward the concept that in a sense, the mind and body are one. That doesn't eliminate the concept of the conscious, unconscious or subconscious minds; they are very real and important parts that keep us alive and define who we are.

Every thought we have creates a chemical reaction that is represented somewhere in our body.[11] When I work with a fibromyalgia client for example, they have often times dealt with significant discomfort for years.

In hypnosis, while interacting with the subconscious mind, I teach them how to minimize stress and achieve greater comfort levels, all because they learn how to control their thoughts. The positive thoughts and expectation of comfort develops into a reality in their body.

If I were to ask you to close your eyes and visualize your car or a particular room where you live, you would likely be able to recall and possibly imagine what they look like. Yet, if I asked you to visualize your mind, what comes up? Chances are, you might have a blank or associate your mind with a picture of a brain.

The human brain is an extremely complex creation with many significant parts. Science has studied and continues to map and study the brain. Yet, no one is able to create a viable picture or say with certainty where the conscious, unconscious or subconscious minds are actually located. Rather than attempt to provide a detailed description that could likely change as new discoveries are found, here's my belief on the interaction between the parts of the mind and our physical responses.

We live each day with the conscious mind. It's always thinking with a critical nature. This critical observer constantly makes judgments about our environment. When an experience occurs, whether it is love or kindness giving a positive feeling, or discomfort with a negative feeling, those sensations are generated in the unconscious mind sending signals to the subconscious. At the same time, they are sending physical responses throughout the body. When the subconscious receives these signals, they are stored to determine future responses, beliefs, and behaviors.

6

The Subconscious Mind

The subconscious mind can determine how you respond to an event based on prior experiences or ingrained beliefs. A powerful tool I use to help neutralize the negative impact of experiences or beliefs is the regression. Important Point: As a Christian, I do not conduct "Past Life" regressions. Scripture states that we were, "*appointed once to die*"[12] so I work with the life of the client sitting in the chair in front of me.

THE JUMPING DOG

The mother of an adolescent girl contacted me because her daughter would freeze in fear and have panic attacks near any unleashed animal. Years earlier, the girl had a small dog that died. Her parents felt it best to allow her time to grieve over the pet and move on.

Five years later the parents decided to get the girl a new puppy.

As puppies are, this little dog was excitable and would jump up at the girl trying to get attention and play. The girl would instantly switch to a panic mode and sometimes climb upon a chair to get away from the small animal.

The girl was raised in a safe and healthy environment with a family that loved her. She was outgoing, happy, loving, smart and involved in a number of school and sports activities. The panicked behavior that appeared around the dog, was totally inconsistent with the rest of her life.

The parents brought her to me to help free her from the paralyzing fear. In our first session, I led the girl into a comfortable state of hypnosis. It was important in this first session to show her she can be successful in hypnosis and help build her confidence levels around the dog.

In an earlier chapter, I discussed how the subconscious mind is non-judgmental and literal. When this part of the mind accepts suggestion (children are very suggestible), the subsequent beliefs and feelings experienced by the subconscious mind can support healthy behaviors in life.

Using a creative visualization process and the powerful imagination within her mind, I had the girl (with her imagination) go to a place at home where her dog is typically found. She described in detail the living room and the dog resting on the floor near the piano.

I asked her to sit on the floor a few feet away from the dog and look in her eyes. *What do you see when you look in her eyes?* I asked. After some back and forth she told me her dog is a good dog, happy and lovable.

She came to realize that her dog has feelings just like her. In the same way that she needs love, sometimes her little puppy also needs love. I asked her if she wanted to pet the dog. She said, "*Yes*", and then (still in hypnosis) went over and began to pet the puppy.

She described how the puppy felt smooth and it made her feel good to pet her and show her love. Because she allowed her subconscious mind to experience loving and petting the puppy, it was an easy step in her normal waking state to follow through and make it real. That afternoon, she began to bond and pet the dog.

Why did this happen in the first place to a healthy, happy girl that had no indication of a fear of animals? While the parents were happy with her new relationship with the dog, the work wasn't done. We needed to find the cause of the underlying emotional trigger that brought her to a place of fear in the first place. The next session was a time for a regression.

THE REGRESSION

When we experience fear or other uncomfortable feelings, what are those? While not intended to be a trick question, they are "Feelings". Every thought creates a chemical reaction that appears as a feeling somewhere. In our second session, I had her bring up that uncomfortable feeling that she doesn't like when she became upset around the dog.

When connecting with that feeling, we can tell the subconscious mind to follow it back to an earlier time when she experienced those feelings. In hypnosis, this is what we call an "Affect Bridge". We are taking that feeling (or affect) and following along a bridge in time to a place where it began.

There were a few stops as we went back, but for this discussion, I'll talk about the place where her fears began. We stopped at five-years of age. The girl described in detail a day where she and her brother were playing ball in the driveway. They were having a good time and then a dog ran up to her.

The dog began jumping at her and nipping at her right hand and arm - not viciously, just trying to get the ball out of her hand to play. Even so, it was scary enough for a five-year-old to think she would be hurt. While the dog eventually ran off, this is a picture of how quickly our subconscious mind can take an emotionally-packed thought and turn it into a belief.

There's another process we can use to help neutralize the emotional event. For the sake of brevity, I'll just say that using the knowledge and experiences of the girl (in her older age), she can help coach the younger, scared child through the event so that she'll feel safe.

After having the five-year-old go through the event two more times, she felt fine, knowing she won't need to react fearfully when situations like this occur in the future.

During this process, the subconscious mind is paying attention and making healthy behavioral adjustments. Fear by itself is not a bad thing; at times it's a healthy warning signal. Given the new insights of having revisited the event, the girl can now respond confidently, rather than reacting fearfully.

Here's an interesting point: when the subconscious mind followed the uncomfortable "feeling" back, it was in her lower right arm and hand, the same hand the dog nipped at, trying to get the ball years earlier.

Since the subconscious mind holds all memories, feelings, and beliefs, this is a good example of how interacting with this part of the mind in hypnosis in a sense allows an undo button. We can never change the past. Yet, we can help a person strengthen their future.

CREATING A HABIT

Hypnosis is a great tool to assist a person who feels captive to a negative habit. Most habits are the result of an emotional trigger. When we have an uncomfortable feeling, we want to make it go away. Rather than deal with it directly, people make a choice to cover it with something else. Simply stated, the bad feeling could be fear, anger, loneliness, boredom, sadness or any other uncomfortable condition.

The internal processing could be something like, "He (or she) really made me mad. I'm better than that! I'm going to have a [candy bar, drink, cigarette or some other covering behavior] and take my mind off of it." Then, when the next negative feeling comes along, you go right back into the, "I'll cover it with something else" behavior. Now granted, I admit that this is a pretty simplistic example but realistically, the feeling-to-response mode is sometimes that direct.

The choice to cover a negative situation or feeling with an unhealthy behavior took your mind off it for a bit, but each time this happens, you solidify a habit. This cycle repeats itself and your subconscious mind says, *"Okay, you feel this way? Then go smoke, drink, eat or do something to cover the bad feelings."* This message is sent, initiating an action and a habit is created. Each time you revisit this cycle, the habit gets stronger.

Certainly, there are opportunities for good choices like exercise, drinking water, meditation, or engaging in a creative outlet. These are healthier options. Unfortunately, people that try to cover negative triggers tend to cover them with negative habits.

It would appear as though the subconscious mind intentionally wants to mess up your life. This is not true. The subconscious mind utilizes learned behaviors to cover negative feelings with something else as a means to protect you. In the same way you were kept from finding a tree in highway hypnosis, the subconscious mind protects you based on learned behaviors to environmental situations or feelings.

A person can neutralize negative habits or behaviors by recognizing the feeling-to-response mode and then choosing to take action. For many people, willpower alone can stop the habit. Yet, if the underlying emotional triggers that caused the habit are not dealt with, many people re-engage in the habit or start a different one. A person caught up in this cycle generally starts to see a distorted view of themselves. As the habit grows stronger, their confidence levels decrease.

HOW HYPNOSIS CAN HELP

Hypnosis is a natural, drug-free option to interact with the subconscious mind. When a person is guided to a place of focused concentration, it is a natural process to transition into a state of hypnosis. At that point, we can interact with the subconscious mind to see things in a clearer perspective. In a sense, we bypass the judgmental conscious mind (or critical factor) that chose to engage in the habit or covering behavior in the first place.

Once the conscious mind is out of the way, a renewing begins that allows a person to have greater insights and confidence through positive suggestion to the subconscious. In the chapters ahead we'll look at a few more situations where hypnosis brought safe, life-changing results to people in need.

·

PART 2

HYPNOSIS
&
THE CHURCH

7

Flaming Arrows

Life as a Christian hypnotist sometimes comes with an underlying expectation of being an open target for judgmental opinion and personal attacks. The short stories below describe incidents where a lack of understanding of scripture or hypnosis (or both) precipitated unkind action as an excuse for religious zeal.

What they are really saying is, *"Don't do good if it's counter to what I've adopted as a belief based on someone else's opinion."* What do I mean by that? Obviously to a large extent, I'm speaking in generalities as there are people in the world that exercise due diligence and make their own opinions by looking at facts. Our society today is blessed with technologies and resources that didn't exist 30-years ago. With the ability to conduct massive computations in less than a microsecond, computer technology was intended to make our lives easier and provide answers faster.

Some of these same technologies are now embedded within household appliances, smart homes, cameras, medical devices, automobiles, watches, phones and more. The computational speed and response time intended to allow our lives a bit of breathing room, is now filled with something else packed into our busy schedules. I believe the rapid access to data has over time, diminished the skill set of critical thinking.

When a person needs an answer, where do they go? They "Google" it.[13] I believe the due diligence to research and utilize cognitive abilities are key elements that can define our national and global survival. Yet, some in national or corporate leadership positions today don't think for themselves anymore. They hire researchers to do it for them.

And so it is with the issue of hypnosis amongst many within the church. When I received judgmental opinions or sometimes outright verbal attacks, I asked simple questions to understand their perspective. Yet often times their answers cannot stand to scrutiny.

THE PASTOR'S CURSE

I received a Facebook friend request from a guy that self-identified as a Pastor of a church. I looked at his profile and he seemed like a normal guy. Looking further I saw we had mutual connections so I went ahead and accepted his request. My profile is very clear about who I am and my background, including being a hypnotist.

Because I also maintain a fine art photography site, I thought he connected for that reason. I have followers from all over that view photography, and it just made sense. A short time afterward I received a private message from this guy. To my surprise, he blasted me with an email full of capital letters and exclamation points. He cursed me and used language that I'm not comfortable sharing here, or anywhere else for that matter.

His point of contention was that I practice hypnosis and according to him, I was demon-filled, going to hell and he said that he wants me to suffer for a painful eternity. This attack came from a guy that said he was a Pastor. I don't know what kind of church he is affiliated with but I can assure you that it is not one that shares the gospel message of a loving God who sent His Son to suffer and die on a cross for my sins.

As a Christian, I have a responsibility to love the sinner - not the sin. Granted, some people are tougher to love on some days; it's an ongoing process. When we choose to live in a state of awareness of our thoughts and feelings, over time our relationship with Christ becomes fortified and we can reach a level of spiritual maturity.

There are plenty of days when I'm not such a pleasant peach to be around; I recognize that. On that day when the Pastor cursed me, I felt my buttons being pushed. Yet, I knew that any response would have been fodder for more abuse. The Facebook "Block" button was a better use of moving on.

THE JUDGMENTAL AUNT

In another instance, I worked with a young woman that was on the receiving end of significant abuse. For quite a while she found herself falling into an emotional pit that kept her in a state of fear. After we began working together, she began to see positive changes occurring within her. In her excitement, she blogged about the work we'd done and the new positive perceptions she noticed within herself. I was (and still am) very proud of her.

The changes that came to her were not because of some magical incantation that I did. The change came because she stepped up and recognized that she needed to shed the emotional triggers and negative claws that constantly tried to pull her back downward.

Sometimes friends and family can be our worst source of support. The young woman's Aunt, in my opinion, is a misguided joy stealer. The Aunt rather than be happy for the new positive changes in her niece, wrote her and told her that she had become a slave to sin that would end in death. Wow…now that seriously lacks loving motivation doesn't it? Then, the Aunt began characterizing me in an unkind fashion.

The young woman wrote me and asked that I provide a response. I replied to both the Aunt and the young woman so we were all on the same page. Ironically, my client and I recently discussed the importance of working with Christian practitioners and the need to stay in safe areas before we ever began our work.

I told the aunt that I understand her concerns completely. As a Christian hypnotist, we discussed these matters and I believe it's important to stay in safe areas and avoid anything counter to our faith

I then followed with a detailed response that I felt honored her concerns. I didn't want her to feel as though in my zeal to justify the work I do, that she was being dismissed. Apparently, the Aunt didn't feel the same way and left me wondering if she had even read the reply or was just blinded by preconceived judgment. Her reply was: *"You can't paint the pump handle white and purify the water."*

Given that answer, it was clear that no discussion would open the mind of a person sealed in a box of judgment. Still wanting to give the woman an opportunity to contemplate the issue, I took a lot of time answering the doubts and outright accusations that I'm in some way bad. I provided detail of what hypnosis is and what it is not.

I described how a person has to be careful because there could be some practitioners that operate in areas that Christians might consider questionable. It becomes easy not to see the facts because we cannot see past the board in our own eye when it's held in place by judgment.

The Aunt had no reply, in typical fashion to others who felt confident being the attacker or intending to "educate" me about my perceived flaws. I've found they find solace hiding behind an email when faced with facts and real-life examples of the positive results with hypnosis.

This is why I wrote this book. I want to help people that have been in a victim situation and lead them to a healthy, happy and enriching life. I also want to help educate people to use their own minds and experiences to make a cogent opinion; not what someone else says is good or bad...but based on our own ability to think.

God created our minds and bodies and provided us with opportunities to live a fulfilled life. Sometimes help is needed to show a person they are not damaged goods and they are important, capable and able to have the confidence to live a life containing love, joy, and enrichment.

As I write this I'm reminded of a woman that came to me for help. She had been beaten and abused for over three decades. Her own husband forced her into human trafficking for eight years. I wish I could honestly say this was a unique case, but it's not.

With the steady flow of abuse clients, I'm convinced these crimes are a darker side of our society that occurs with regularity. I can tell you the abusers come from all walks of life, and sometimes they hide behind positions of influence, There's no excuse for their behavior.

This woman had tried conventional therapies and medication for years without success. Just like you and I, she had hopes and dreams as a child. She wanted to be loved, cared for and valued. Yet, she lived in an abusive place where her dreams and self-perceived value were stolen from her. One of the most powerful processes we use in hypnosis is forgiveness work.

During these sessions, we neutralize the power of the abuser and release others who had a hold on the client's life. Then, we emphasize the concept of the client releasing themselves of the self-guilt they've carried. Since working through these processes together, she has been able to forgive her abuser, release herself from the hold he had on her and has since invited Christ into her life.

Which is better? Leaving her with a talk therapist that didn't get to the root of the problem and kept her as a medicated victim…or a freed person who after years, now has joy as a survivor with a new relationship with God?

Those who are so willing to shoot flaming arrows of judgment would do well put aside the need to be opinionated. There are real people with real issues, most often caused by the unkindness of others. God didn't create us to live in a state of lack, or fear. We should consider safe and natural processes that allow a person to live with confidence and love.

8

God Makes No Mistakes

As a Christian, I believe God does not make mistakes – people do. Yet, with proper care and feeding a person can live the life they were intended. Relationships can be healed, forgiveness of others and forgiveness of ourselves no longer seems insurmountable, and the effects of stress from traumatic situations can be calmed. We really can be freed from the misdeeds of abusers and our own sense of self-guilt.

People can walk through each day knowing they are capable and kind without the history of poor behaviors by others impacting their lives. The negative self-talk implanted by their own unresolved issues no longer has soil to take root. Have you ever had the negative tape player constantly playing in your head? Of course you have – you're alive. Wouldn't you like to change the station and listen to the good in your life?

When held captive by years of negativity, the only things that grow in our lives are weeds and thorn bushes. Positive interaction with the subconscious mind through hypnosis can quickly bring change in good ways.

RELEASING THE PAST - STRENGTHENING RELATIONSHIPS

Releasing the implants and junk of the past by a parent, teacher or person of influence in a child's life can free them and define a happier, more successful and productive future. This is one reason I like to work with couples before they get married.

If a person preparing for marriage carried the misdeeds of others as a child, as a new spouse, they are that same child, only grown up to an older age. They carry the same negative feelings, fears and confidence problems right into the marriage.

Yet, when a couple opts to clear the past and release their internal garbage prior to sealing their lives together, they can spread the wealth of peace, and enjoy a lasting partnership based on love and kindness for generations.

Our histories, beliefs and false perceptions forced upon us by others take root over time and impact both our relationships and future. Why would anyone enter into a long-term relationship promising to love, cherish, protect, honor and respect each other if their new spouse isn't willing to take the time to clear the baggage beforehand?

What baggage am I talking about? The unresolved hurts, fears, worries, anger, and disappointments. If either (or both) sides of the relationship choose not to get rid of the old junk beforehand, then they are willingly bringing those same issues into the new marriage.

Eventually, both sides will subconsciously be measuring their new spouse against old history. Is that fair to them? By their choice not to address their past, they are saying:

"Oh Honey...I love you so much. I want to spend my life with you. Here...help me carry around my bag of trash."

That's absurd. Many problems exist because people don't address them and pretend they will go away. Unresolved issues carry their own bag of manure with them. Something will always grow out of it and chances are it will stink.

Granted, most people don't know about hypnosis and they have no idea that it can clear the old hurts and pave a loving path for the future. New couples fall in love, get caught up in the moment, spend thousands of dollars on a wedding and blame their new spouse if things don't work out later.

Now don't get me wrong. I'm not against love and marriage or making the wedding day an important memory. What I'm saying is each one pledging their life and love should look closely at themselves to ensure they are giving their new spouse the very best.

Inherently, we know when there's something under the surface that needs addressing. Knowingly walking into a lifetime relationship, hoping the past will never surface is irresponsible. Hypnosis can help resolve those hurts of the past and strengthen relationships.

PUTTING CHILDREN ON A SUCCESSFUL PATH

In the same way that a marriage is strengthened by resolving the old history, their children can prosper as well. This is an important point here. Too many parents miss opportunities with their children.

During the early years, a child's brainwaves fluctuate in and out of highly suggestible states. This important time should not be missed. It's the time to teach them how to love or be loved, and how to be a contributing part of society. This is a time when children should be encouraged and shown they can be confident.

As scripture tells us, *"Train a child in the way he should go: and when he is old, he will not depart from it."*[14] God knew long ago in the writing of His word that we can impact our youth in positive ways if we are responsible and take action.

Look at our society today with the vast number of latch-key kids. Left on their own with little encouragement or mentoring it's no wonder crime and societal issues continue to rise in our nation.

You don't need to look too far in the daily news to see youth bullying, gang activities, drug use, sexual assaults, and suicide. It becomes easy to sit on the sidelines and say these kids were bad and they got what they asked for. That's just not true.

They need love and care and respect and a person willing to show them they are important. Yet, these kids are not getting the proper care, love and encouragement that strengthens their hearts and minds. They need to be mentored and loved and told they can be successful. I'm not talking about the *"Every child gets a trophy"* mentality - that's the lazy way out.

God created us as emotional beings with an internal need to interact in a positive way. Now at this point of this chapter, you might be wondering, *"What does this have to do with hypnosis?"* It has everything to do with it.

Take another look the paragraph above where I talked about the natural brainwave state that occurs in our youth. This happens because God created us all to be receptors and absorb information as children. The brain frequencies that occur, interact directly with the subconscious mind, implanting knowledge and perception of ourselves, and the world. This is the same state that would interact with *your* subconscious mind if you were in my hypnosis chair.

When I'm working with a person that is fearful or faced abuses or unkindness that destroyed a person's self-perception, I take them to that same natural state to help them live a life, confident and happy.

Looking back on the children around us, they don't need a Hypnotist or a person like me; they naturally go in and out of that receptive state. They need parents, other family, teachers or influencers that step up and encourage the children who are the potential leaders of our nation's future.

The problem with many parents today is they are uninvolved, self-absorbed children in larger bodies that never resolved their issues prior to marriage or childbirth. Years ago we used to hear the term, "Trickle-down economics". I believe parenting today in many ways could be called, "Trickle-down irresponsibility" for not addressing negative influences of the past.

It's important to note that I'm not pointing fingers at others without including myself into the mix. When I got married, I was 22-years old without any understanding of positive living, and I sure had plenty of bad history I was carrying.

I had no understanding of hypnosis or how to be a positive contributor or a partner in a marriage. When our daughter was born, it was apparent that I knew even less. I'm not saying that hypnosis is the only modality that can resolve past hurt, perceptions, and triggers.

I'm sure there will be new discoveries ahead as brain science research continues. I can say however; hypnosis offers the fastest change with some permanency that I've seen. So far in this chapter, we looked at two of the many potential examples where hypnosis can help people resolve stumbling blocks in life, or prepare young lives for success.

In both cases, hypnosis is a natural and helpful resource to find the positive. God created our minds and bodies. He also created the ability to slow down with focused concentration. God does not make mistakes and using the natural abilities instilled into our lives, we can live happy, productive lives.

9

Judgment In The Church

I believe some people choose to live in a state of uninformed judgment claiming hypnosis is of the devil. On the surface, it might appear easier for a person to dig their heels into the ground, staying planted in one place, without truly knowing why they hold those beliefs.

I've been told that I'm, *"obviously not a Christian"* because I believe in hypnosis. Really? How can a person even pretend to know the state of my heart or my relationship with Christ? Particularly when their own beliefs appear coated in the murkiness of their judgmental, ill-informed heart? Instead of criticizing and denigrating Christian hypnotists, they would do well to become informed of the miraculous mind and body that God created. I believe it's a huge error to believe that our Lord was incapable of creating a perfectly planned mind and body, able to enjoy healing and renewal through a natural process.

If the critical-minded were willing to take time to understand the safe and natural processes that leads a person to personal success, that same condemning person might have to look closer at themselves. I find it ironic that we worship our Savior who came and walked on this earth as a carpenter, yet we carry boards of judgment in our own eyes.

As humans, we are imperfect because mankind walked right into a sinful condition. With that comes judgment and disparate relationships with those around us. I admittedly include myself in this tendency to fall into moments of judgment. Our walk consists of daily steps that can change for good if we recognize our personal condition and do something about it. We sinned – God did Not.

Humans tend to mirror those around us. Take any grouping of people, whether it be a company, organization or a church. Over time, those within the organizational structure become comfortable with their known social dynamic.

I've learned through personal observation if a person strays from the perceived rules of behavior, beliefs or occupation, their level of acceptance diminishes. The person either chooses to conform to expectations, they leave the group or they risk becoming a social outcast.

Such as the Pastor I described on Facebook. I personally have little tolerance of people that point fingers or make judgments against others when they have no understanding of the target of their abuse.

Even more disappointing is when some deflect the issues and claim a religious zeal as justification for their behavior. This failed mindset leading to self-justified behaviors is a problematic condition becoming prevalent throughout our nation and across the world.

Some people should just wear a T-shirt that says, *"I don't want you to improve yourself if it's done without my approval."* It's no wonder that our government, politics, social issues and moral compass have gone awry.

I've seen victims of significant challenge and abuse have their self-care and recovery efforts inhibited by judgmental people that don't approve of hypnosis. Instead of loving and encouraging the person to a restored life, roadblocks are tossed in their way.

Sometimes these roadblocks exist within the church. With no foundational knowledge of hypnosis, they pull out their tool bags full of gossip, rumor, slander, or exclusion, planting doubt of a person's ability to be saved if they see a hypnotist.

I believe this is spiritually dangerous. If a person claiming Christianity scolds or embarrasses a person seeking care, or they tell them they'll go to hell for seeing a hypnotist, how does that help them overcome the years of abuse, lack of confidence, or the free-floating fear they live with each day?

Now, please don't interpret what I'm saying to suggest there's a consortium of churches with a mission to ban hypnosis. That's not the case. I can tell you that just about any hypnotist in practice over a year has likely seen potential clients talked away from care, or the hypnotist themselves has personally felt the sting of judgment.

Fortunately, I'm happy to say that I attend a solid Bible church that accepts me for my desire to live a life that honors God, without judgment of the work I do.

SORROWS IN THE CHURCH

Our churches are full of people carrying deep, deep sorrows, fears, or believe they are unworthy of being saved or living the life God planned for them. Within our churches are men and women who faced abuse or molestation as children.

There are people carrying sorrows because they never met a biological parent and they internally wonder who they are. There are those who grieve over sons, daughters or other familial ties through sickness, suicide, crime or war.

There are people who fear death and they've never felt whole or accepted. These same people lived their lives constantly being fed the message that they are failures.

People that have carried the hurts and disappointments throughout their lives are intuitive; they recognize judgment immediately. In the face of the familiar, how can a person live a life with a true relationship with Jesus? How can they look forward to crossing over to Heaven when they struggle to live with themselves?

Where is it that scripture says we have the right to love some, as long as they look, think or act according to our own judgmental opinions? When was the last time you prayed that God would intervene in a person's life to surround them with situations or people to bring them to a saving knowledge of Christ? Or perhaps, to intervene and heal their hurting heart, even if it's outside our comfort zone? Chances are if you're a Christian, you've prayed that first prayer dozens, or hundreds of times.

Yet, we struggle with that second prayer because that would be allowing God to operate outside the safe parameters we've set for

Him. I'm guilty of that myself as are many of us.

Our mortal minds are incapable of seeing the great possibilities of God. His own word says "My thoughts are higher than your thoughts; my ways are higher than your ways." God created the mind and body, and using hypnosis helps strengthen a person. We don't have the right to say, "*No…God, just zap them and heal them. Don't use a Christian hypnotist to help strengthen our flock in the church.*"

Self-admission moment: I'm not about to pretend that I've finally conquered a tendency of viewing God's ability as something operating only within my lens of the world. Walking in faith is a daily practice and every day I learn unique nuances of the way God operates in my life and those around me.

In my practice, there are places I just won't go as a hypnotist. In a later chapter, I'll give further detail of those areas. I've seen incredible life change where people were able to release themselves from some of the darkest, abusive places.

I also know that God had His hand in my finding hypnosis when I didn't even believe in it. If you're a person that still has their heels dug into the ground with the opinion that hypnosis is bad, here's some advice from my own faith walk with God: I've seen the power of God operate the most dynamically when I invite Him to act as He sees fit and I get out of His way.

A DISMISSIVE BROTHER

A couple years into my practice I was selected as a faculty member to present at the National Guild of Hypnotists annual convention in Marlborough, Massachusetts. My topic was, *"Reaching out to Law*

Enforcement, Responders, and Our Military". Having served in two military services before earning my retirement, and serving in a law enforcement capacity as a federal investigator, I understand their challenges.

With the upcoming presentation, I admit I was a bit nervous. My audience were peers with decades of professional experience more than me; many traveled in from all over the globe.

I did what any Christian should do in that instance - I reached out for prayer support to a person I respected and was confident would understand the importance of the topic. Here was a guy that's known me for a long time. He's retired law enforcement and leads a men's group where men pray and support other men.

I contacted him and asked a simple thing: *"Would you pray that I'll be able to get the point across to the audience? I'd like to see other practitioners reach out and support those who serve our communities, and support them with stress management."* I wasn't even talking about hypnosis. The presentation focused on stress management.

I was a bit surprised by his *conditional* response. He indicated that he would pray but *first*, he said he wanted me to send him something about hypnosis and Christianity. Even though we already discussed this in person months earlier, I told him I'd send the info.

That evening I spent a lot of time detailing what hypnosis is, what it is not, the misperceptions and the reality. I then described the circumstances which drew me to hypnosis. I then sent him a private message on Facebook, telling him I sent the info to his personal account for easier reading.

A couple hours later I received a Facebook reply. His reply: *"Is it long?"* That was a second indicator of where this prayer request was going. It goes without saying that actually opening the email would help a person determine its length.

Days went by without a reply, a week - no reply. I went to the convention, presented and returned home. A couple weeks later, I received a Facebook message from him. I quickly opened it, hoping to hear how he supported me in prayer to help expand stress management services to those who serve.

His reply was a single one-word email: *"Thanks"*. That was our last communication. During the succeeding months after the convention, he never asked how it went nor was there any indication of prayer support.

I have absolutely no confidence that my prayer request was shared or even considered with the men's group. I wish I could say this disappointment was an anomaly, but it's not.

Even while writing this, I find it a little hurtful to think that my request was dismissed by a guy that leads a men's group that prays for and supports other men in the church. My requested prayer support first was conditional with, *"I'll pray for you IF you do this…"*, then being told that after complying with his request, it wasn't even worth opening the email to read.

This dismissive attitude divides, it does not build nor strengthen. I believe my hope for prayer support was dismissed because I was known as a Christian hypnotist and it didn't fall in line with a comfortable, non-challenging or effortless request.

It's my understanding that the old hymn, *"Onward Christian Soldiers"*[15] represents a unified choice to stand and support each other. Yet, some without an understanding of the incredible life-changing help a Christian hypnotist can bring, choose to live with a sense of justification for irresponsible behavior. Truly disappointing.

Now I recognize and fully admit that had I followed scripture to the letter, I should have gone to him and let him know I was hurt by it. In those succeeding months, I considered speaking with him and recognized a sense of avoidance, indicating he didn't want to talk and I saw no value in trying to push the issue. I eventually left and found another church where all people are seen as important, rather than the titles they hold.

It's important to clarify that I don't believe this individual is a failed Christian or his faith is in some way flawed. That would be inappropriate for me to make such a judgmental assumption since I have no way to know another person's walk with God.

Yet, I write about it here, not to call out an individual, but to show how people are hurt – not just in the church, but throughout the world. People are dismissed and sometimes there's an expectation that poor behaviors should be ignored because we're a brother or sister in Christ. That's not a hypnosis issue – it's a church issue.

When things like this occur, people receive the incorrect message that they are unimportant. It becomes very easy when we live in the world to act like the world. When this happens in the church, it drives a wedge between the Gospel message and those that need to hear it.

Looking at the broader view, as humans, we naturally seek areas of comfort and allow avoidance to rule our actions (or inactions). Had this man gone to his group and asked for prayer support, someone might have asked if I was that, "Hypnotist guy". Then, he might have found himself in the uncomfortable position of validating the value of my stress management presentation. All that said, I believe he's a great guy that loves God and means to do well. I believe he might have found himself in an uncomfortable spot when I asked for his support.

There are many places in the Bible where people chose avoidance. I don't know for sure, but I can only imagine that Jonah probably didn't like seafood. God told him to preach against the city of Nineveh, then Jonah chose avoidance and ran away. Through that avoidance, he ended up in the belly of a big fish.[16]

I believe that's how God works sometimes, taking the very things we want to avoid to teach us lessons and show us the goodness that God has in store for us. I'm certainly guilty of avoiding the uncomfortable at times and each day I learn new ways to make better choices. The Christian walk is a faith exercise where we learn to strengthen our spiritual muscles.

STOLEN OPPORTUNITIES

A hypnotist friend in New Hampshire told me a disheartening story. In an effort to reach out to potential clients and be help to her community, she bought airtime with a Christian radio station for a few short commercials. The audios were recorded and she paid all the fees for the airtime.

Shortly after airing, donors to the station began threatening to pull their financial support if her paid time slots were not taken off the air. Rather than honor a commitment to air the paid advertisements, they relented to the donors and the ads were pulled.

She focused her small business on helping people. Her goal was to provide a drug-free, holistic option to those in need of help. I believe it's safe to say those who become Hypnotists don't do it for wealth. The positive change and life restoration they see each day is the driving force to do this work.

Hypnosis is a caregiving profession and we do it because we want to make a difference in people's lives. In the New Hampshire case, a few people made threats and acted out of their own ignorance of hypnosis, effectively removing caregiving opportunities from their own community.

10

The Full Armor Of God

As a Christian, I understand the value of memorizing scripture. When we do, we insert it into our mind and heart as a reinforcement of God's truth in our lives.

When we need comfort, His word is like a warm coat on a cold snowy day, holding us close with a sense of safety and security. On good days when life is going smoothly, His word is a validation of His love, care and answer to prayer.

Yet, when the storms come (and they do), His word is a critical shield for us that protects and gives us hope. We can hang onto scripture as a lifeline, allowing it to take root deep into our subconscious minds for recall and application when needed.

In the early 1980's, I was building a commercial photography business in New Orleans. One morning on the way to a photo shoot, I was rear-ended by an 18-wheeler hauling drill pipe. I can still replay the accident in my mind as a time-lapse film; the screeching of brakes and the loud explosive sound of the impact.

It's amazing how the subconscious mind holds every experience.

My business was gone and I was laid up for quite a while. In the ensuing months, life and my perception of it continued to spiral downward until I realized my plans and efforts weren't working. They were as scripture tells us, *"like filthy rags"*.[17]

With this new awareness, I asked Jesus to forgive me and save me. Being a new Christian gave me a new heart. Yet it didn't change my circumstances and it didn't change my past. When we become saved, we are given an eternal future with a savior who loves and cares for us. Yet, salvation doesn't automatically give us a free ticket to some paradise, free of challenge and struggle. As a baby Christian, I needed to grow and mature, learning to stand firm in my faith.

During that time, I remember latching onto a scripture that strengthened me and gave me a hope for the future:

> *"Consider it joy my brethren, when you encounter various trials, knowing that the testing of your faith produces endurance. And let endurance have its perfect result, so that you will be perfect and complete, lacking in nothing."*[18]

Even today, decades later, that word lives within me stronger than ever because the years allowed me to see God at work in my life and those around me.

My point here is that I'm not trying to pretend that I'm some spiritual warrior. I'm a guy that sees the need to keep my faith connected as an active part of my life. There should be no separation.

In my practice, I am mindful that the successes I see with my clients are the result of God's leading and blessing. It's my goal to help my clients regain a life stolen from them through years of abuse or false perceptions.

I sometimes wonder if some in the church really believe God created a mind and body capable of living a full life of love, joy, and peace. I've seen some within the church reciting scripture, and that's great. Yet, these same people have levied judgment at me for working to help, and against victims of abuse who sought help from the church. The result is twofold: those seeking spiritual help either depart the church or they question their reasons for being there.

Judgment is a dangerous thing. Through judgment some are expected to carry the worlds' garbage and live a lesser life by complying with uninformed notions of what hypnosis is or isn't. The church should be focused on strengthening those around us - both within and outside our church doors. We need to share a truth: *"While we were yet sinners, Christ died for all of us."*[19]

I'm not saying judgment against hypnosis is a widespread problem in the church. Yet, it does exist. I've been on the receiving end of it and I don't like it.

As a Christian this frustrates me because the message of some is:

"It doesn't matter if you live a life of fear, worry, anger, or sadness. We think hypnosis is bad, so just stay in your sad condition."

What incentive is there for a hurting, unsaved person to make an eternal decision for Christ when some in the church expect them to stay stuck? Who are we as Christians to make this judgment?

Christ died for us so that we can share the message of His grace and love and show the world they no longer have to be captive to the physical, spiritual or environmental evils. When I discuss hypnosis, I'm not saying it is *the* tool. I'm saying it is *a* tool. It allows us to bring goodness to lives burdened by emotional triggers and false perceptions that others have placed upon them.

THE SPIRITUAL ARMOR

In Ephesians 6:10-17, it discusses the need for us to put on the *"Full armor of God"*.[20] We are not told to put on the armor just in case something bad happens. We know there are evils in the world. Scripture says to put on the armor of God *when* the day of evil comes.[21] Some may be quick to say I'm misquoting this passage but please stick with me here. It's probably obvious by now that I believe that since God created our minds and bodies, we should focus them for His good.

Verse 14 tells us to stand firm with the *"belt of truth"* around our waist.[22] In my practice, I can safely say that every client has been affected (including myself) by false truths in our lives. Haven't you? Of course you have.

We've all heard those stories of not being good enough, thin enough, smart enough, capable enough, fast enough, or just fill in the blank with the false story you heard about not being enough of something. Those are the batteries that reside in our minds and turn on the negative tape player each day.

When we interact with the subconscious mind, we gain a clearer view of what truth looks like. When we know truth, life still requires effort, but we have talents, skills, and abilities. As the negative noise fades, we are in a better place to hear what God is telling us and live the life intended for us.

The passage in Ephesians tells us to wear the *"breastplate of righteousness"*.[23] I believe all righteousness comes from God and when we free our lives of false beliefs, we can walk closer to the standard that God set for us.

We can walk in readiness to share and enjoy the gospel of peace. We are abler to develop a relationship in a peaceful environment than one of struggle. The relationship I'm talking about is a relationship with the God who sent His Son to die for you and me.

It is through this relationship that we learn, experience and develop a level of faith. We are told to take up the shield of faith to extinguish the arrows of the evil one. Ultimately the evil one is the devil that fills people's lives with false beliefs.

Yet for this discussion of my clients, the evil one might have been a parent who neglected to love or care for them. The evil one could have been a relative that abused them in some way, a stranger, a neighbor, teacher or some other person that physically, emotionally or psychologically caused long-lasting damage.

Many times, the evil one is the same client aiming self-abuse toward themselves. Over time they chose to believe a good life is for someone else so they feed their minds with negative messages of guilt and incompetence. In hypnosis, we build a client's ability to choose faith over fear by neutralizing the power of the evil one.

Ephesians tells us to take the *"Helmet of salvation and the sword of the spirit, which is the word of God"*.[24] As a church, we should be interested. Actually, we should be *more* than interested. People are interested in football or music or art or stamp collecting. Yet, none of those save. We should be *driven* to help those around us be the best they can be. We should be purpose-driven to help others live a life that blesses rather than one diminished and weakened.

When a person knows what God did for them and accepts Christ into their life, they can confidently wear the helmet of salvation. Armed with these important elements of knowledge and protection, they are empowered with the sword of the Spirit to stand and walk confidently.

The best fruit comes from a tree that has been pruned. I work with lots of clients that feel lost and hurt, believing they are broken goods. When we begin the pruning process, cutting away the false beliefs, we allow new growth.

Some of the most successful life-change agents are those that have experienced the greatest challenge. Then, through their own emersion into a new life, they subsequently helped others. If a person carrying emotional sadness with them each day is prevented from moving forward, their potential joy fades away like lost film in an old camera - never developed, never seen, and never enjoyed.

In my experience, clients who struggle with a negative self-view or self-talk are often held back by emotional implants from experiences or negative suggestions. If we as a Christian community seek to strengthen a person's spiritual health and ultimately the strength of our congregations, I believe it's crucial their emotional health is clear of roadblocks that divert a person away from spiritual maturity. I work at the emotional level and I do that through hypnosis, a safe and natural process.

I believe the narrative found in Ephesians of the full armor of God is relevant today just as it was written 2,000 years ago. While the world is full of evil we don't have to fear it, or hide away as a recluse; as Christians, we have a covering.

In Psalm 91 we are told:

> *"He will command His angels concerning you to guard you in all your ways".*[25]

If we could see with spiritual eyes for only three seconds, we would see how God shields us from a multitude of threats every second of every day. Frankly, I believe if we actually saw those threats, we'd drop of a heart attack or be frozen in fear. Fortunately, we don't have to see the reality of that darker world when we have God's protection. I believe helping a person live confidently to see they were created in love, opens the door to long-lasting spiritual decisions and wearing that helmet of salvation.

If you're a Christian leader and my words sting or a church member and you're unsure how to respond if the issue of hypnosis comes up, I implore you to educate yourself. Scripture says, *"Study to show yourself approved".*[26] When a person pursues knowledge and avoids judgment, they can act in love.

It's important to know what hypnosis is, and what it is not. I understand the concerns of some in the church. I believe the worries are precipitated by practices of non-Christian hypnotists, stage performances, and Hollywood. I'll dig further into finding the right practitioners and why in the pages ahead.

11

A Church Persona

In a sense, our churches have an active marketing and branding program. I know that sounds critical and that's not my intent, but it makes sense. It's important to be presented as a place for all; a place where people will find loving, caring members; a place where families can feel safe; a place where they can find out about GOD and their place in the world; a place where perhaps they can be a part of helping others. All that is good. In fact, that's what the church should be - that, and so much more. The conditions of this world have millions feeling in a quandary, unsure if, how and where they fit. They need help.

Some carry shame from earlier years when they felt trapped and perhaps had an abortion or were caught up in unhealthy habits. So many within our churches desperately need love and kindness so they wrap themselves with a persona that appears acceptable. All the while, the deep emotional, physical and psychological injuries fester within their inner being.

Those filling our churches are real people with real issues. All of us who now have a relationship with Jesus got here because we did a good job of screwing up our lives. We reached a point where we realized the old ways won't work and old habits led us in the wrong direction. Yet, many still deal with the negative internal messages that compound stress and the emotional damage, that causes physical deterioration.

Some congregations project the appearance that those in the church live a near-perfect life without struggle, as if they have arrived at their destination. The reality is, life is an ongoing hike and we never arrive anywhere until we reach the eternal destination we chose. Our churches are full of people who either carry or have carried a deep sadness or fear that clutches their very core.

Fears, doubts, and a skewed self-perception can make a person worry if they are really saved. Granted, none are worthy of salvation, it is a gift. Yet, our burdens and our past hamper our ability to accept and enjoy that saving grace. It's my belief that many of us in the church often worry whether we are truly living the life God predestined for us, and few know true peace.

Bring up the conversation of how we will all stand before the Lord one day and it can become very uncomfortable, very quickly. I admit I fear that day. Scripture tells us, *"The fear of the Lord is the beginning of knowledge."*[27] That knowledge of who He is in relation to our sinful state can be scary. All sin is sin and we all know the times when we really blew it. We struggle to forgive ourselves and those around us. God's Word says the He (not us) forgives our sin, *"and remembers it no more."*[28]

I believe it's smart to have a healthy fear of the Lord. Yet, we also should remember that His word is true and we can live a happy, loving and successful life under His grace.

In my work as a Christian hypnotist, I work with people to help them shed the false beliefs that they are broken vessels, never to be filled with love, joy or confidence. Most arrive at my office from outside the church; many from within.

How are these people who struggle with their own identity, beating themselves up each day with current or past situations ever going to live a life of happiness? If they struggle with earthly relationships from fears, how can they reach a peaceful place and relationship with Jesus?

Granted, all things are possible with God. He can create situations leading to a salvation decision in an instant. Change happens. Why would a person who struggled through life believing the negative labels thrown at them choose to stay there?

When a person professing to be a scriptural mentor, tells a person that hypnosis is sacrilegious, they not only impede a life of freedom; I believe they risk preventing a salvation decision. If we can't get along with each other in the church, how can we possibly think we can set a living example for the world to follow?

In my experience, these *"words of wisdom"* they share are based on something they might have heard someone else say without any self-effort to learn the facts. It's important to have good scriptural mentors to lead and grow those finding their faith walk with God. It's also important to know what you are talking about.

When a person acts without knowledge and opts to judge, they might do well to focus on the board sticking out of their own eye, rather than small splinters in the eye of those seeking help. Instead of appearing that we have it all down, I believe we need to live real…step up and admit our faults so that we can help real people with real issues experience the saving grace God provides for us.

12

The Right Hypnotist

Should Christians see a Hypnotist? If a person has underlying emotional triggers that push them toward unhealthy habits, or they struggle with confidence issues, sure; hypnosis is a safe way to find a resolution quickly.

As a Christian, I believe it's important that you know about the practitioner you're seeing. In your area, a non-Christian hypnotist might be your only option because of availability.

When you go to your primary care doctor, optometrist or dentist, you don't first ask them if they are Christian; you seek the best care. You might ask yourself: Since hypnosis is safe and you have control over everything that happens, then what's the big deal?

IS THERE A PROBLEM?

I believe there could be reason for concern, depending on the types of work the practitioner does. I don't want to give the impression that non-Christians should be stereotyped as dangerous - that's backward and inappropriate thinking.

I know hundreds of hypnotists of all levels; many who are not Christians and I trust them because they are professional, well-trained and committed to providing you the best professional care. These non-Christian practitioners utilize their skill as a hypnotist to help you transform unresolved issues that plagued your life. I am proud to know them and would willingly be hypnotized by them myself.

Do you know the right questions to ask to determine if they are well-trained and free of areas counter to our Christian faith? I believe with certainty that hypnosis is a safe and effective, drug-free way to resolve many areas in your life. But do you want someone who delves into the darker spiritual practices? I would say, "Probably not".

This chapter will help prepare you to make a safe and intelligent decision. To be clear, I'll repeat what I said about my optic for this book in the introduction: "I am a Christian before I am a hypnotist." As Christians, you and I have a responsibility to live a life that honors God, shows love and compassion to others, and spreads the gospel throughout the world.

Yet, a practitioner operating outside those parameters could inadvertently invite an unhealthy distraction away from your walk with Jesus. Others advertise outright practices contrary to Christianity. Do I believe they are intentionally working in darker spiritual realms to counter Christianity? No. I don't think so.

Our society is full of "searchers" looking for answers that might seem to work for them. During their search, they tend to fill their lives with information to satisfy a need addressing their current temporal space, rather than seek a long-lasting, eternal relationship.

To be fair to them, I remember very well, those early years searching for a career, wealth and solutions for my day-to-day life. I never thought or considered that giving my life to a Savior far exceeded in value anything that I was capable of doing myself.

As a non-Christian, it was unimportant to me at that time and I was satisfied with any small gains I could achieve on my own. I think these practitioners believe they are providing a good service even if they try to keep Jesus outside their door.

This is precisely what gives some in the church fodder to attack hypnosis. When some practitioners operate within dark spiritual places, I believe those with objections have every right to express their concerns.

AVOIDING UNNECESSARY BATTLES

I know some practitioners that work in areas I find a bit uncomfortable. Yet, they are kind, loving and intelligent people. In the same way that some in the church are determined to believe hypnosis is bad, practitioners who do this work believe what they are doing is good. This creates an, *"us against them"* perspective and with both sides being skeptical or offended by the other. This doesn't fix anything.

If you're reading this book as a Christian, let's bear in mind that before we found faith and made a salvation decision, there were a lot of facts we did not know. There are many very experienced, non-Christian practitioners that may be in the same place in their faith walk. This is a good time to pray for those non-Christian practitioners rather than dismiss hypnosis completely.

Christians have likely read about Paul in the Book of Acts. In his religious zeal, he believed Christians were bad and he had them rounded up and sent to prison for their faith. He was content with his persecution of Christians until he himself had a personal experience with Jesus.[29] Then, he changed his ways and became a leading author of New Testament texts and an unrelenting missionary for Christ.

If God could save Paul, and He can save you and me as the sinners we are, and He has the ability to save every other person on this earth, then we as Christians have a duty to pray for those we feel are placing themselves in spiritual jeopardy.

I don't poke them in the eye with my beliefs; I share my faith and perspectives. It's better to treat them with love and care. It's through relationships that we avoid unnecessary battles and plant good seed in their lives.

LOOKING CLOSER AT THE PRACTITIONER

It's important to know the training, experience, and types of work done by the practitioner. How do you do that? Nowadays, most businesses have a website. Carefully review the pages, their services, the Frequently Asked Questions (FAQs) and any client reviews.

If there are any areas for concern, they will likely show up in your search. If you're still unsure, pick up the phone and talk to them, or send an email with questions.

Here are just a few questions to help your understanding of the practitioner:

- What training did they receive and why that trainer?
- Are they Certified by a professional body and what certifications do they hold?
- How long have they been in practice?
- What (if any) professional organizations do they belong to?
- Are there annual training requirements to maintain membership?
- Do they ascribe to a professional Code of Ethics?
- Do they perform "Spiritual" work? If so, have them describe that for you.
- What are their feelings about past life regressions?

OPERATING OUTSIDE THE SCOPE OF PRACTICE

This next section has nothing to do with the faith of the Practitioner as a Christian or non-Christian. This is important because you want someone to work with that is willing to follow a dedicated code of conduct. A quick Internet search can easily return a list of practitioners willing to provide service related to diagnosed medical or psychological conditions.

There are some hypnotists that are licensed health care providers. However, if the Practitioner is not a licensed medical or mental health professional, they should not be treating such conditions unless they receive a referral from a doctor.

Using the National Guild of Hypnotists Code of Ethics as the standard, it says:

"Hypnotists may work with issues related to a medical or mental health disorder only on referral from a properly licensed health care professional."[30]

Now, this is an important point: Hypnotists can and do provide service for a variety of medical issues, and do so legally IF they receive a medical referral from a doctor.

I know this may sound confusing. After all, why would a doctor refer their patient to a non-medical practitioner? It's actually quite common.

The hypnotist provides Complementary Care that supports the doctor's medical approach. Contrary to common belief, the hypnotist is NOT providing Alternative Care.

When a doctor refers someone to me for Fibromyalgia, or stress, or to help with sleep troubles, I'm not diagnosing anything and I'm not prescribing medication of any kind.

A hypnotist helps ordinary, everyday people with ordinary, everyday problems using individual hypnotic techniques.[31] Using this approach, the client can find a level of comfort by teaching them hypnotic techniques that will benefit them, while lessening the patient load for the healthcare professionals.

Many clients will arrive telling me they experience "anxiety". This term has become part of our regular vernacular. Yet, I always ask if they are under the care of a doctor or if they have been formally diagnosed. In almost all cases, the answer to that question is, "No". If they do have a formal medical diagnosis, then I won't see them or address anxiety without a medical referral.

In the same way, I get clients that initially tell me they think they have PTSD. They were never diagnosed and they are not under the care of a doctor. Given that, we most often begin working on stress management, confidence building and I teach them methods to cope with stressful situations.

This work alone can yield wonderful changes in a person's life. If at any point I feel the client is in need of a physical or mental health assessment, I'll stop our sessions and refer them to an appropriate health care provider. Additionally, I won't resume sessions for that issue until a health care provider refers them back to me.

Conversely, I have had doctors refer their PTSD patients to me. As noted above, with a referral, I'm working in cooperation with their doctor – not as an alternative provider.

Pain management is also an area where hypnosis can help as long as there is a referral. Many practitioners advertise they can help with medical issues. If the Practitioner is not a health care provider, their website should say so.

The following is the text on the front page of my Hypnosis website:

> *"I am not a medical or mental health provider. I am a Board Certified Hypnotist trained through the American School of Clinical Hypnosis. I hold a certification through the National Guild of Hypnotists and a Certification as a 5-PATH® Practitioner.*
>
> *If some issues are outside the scope of my practice, I can refer you to those best able to help. I am obligated by an ethical standard to pursue the best care for you and operate within the scope of my training.*
>
> *In many cases, even if you are being seen by a medical professional, I can help you if I receive a medical referral. This is common practice as many doctors refer to certified consulting hypnotists to complement their plan of care."*[32]

This approach makes it clear what my training is, and what it's not. It also clarifies that if issues arise during our sessions that are outside my scope, then I'll refer the client to the best care appropriate for them.

Providing a client with hypnotic techniques helps them reach an optimum level of success. The best practitioners know to operate within the scope of their training and practice.

WHAT ABOUT THEIR FAITH?

According to a Pew Research Center study in 2014, there are millions of people in the U.S. that associate themselves as being a Christian. Of those, 47% attend religious services regularly; 32% participate in prayer or a regular scripture study.[33] It's as though there's a belief that says, "Well, I don't worship the devil so that means that I must be a Christian." Others tend to call themselves an agnostic, while others don't know what they believe.

Throughout our global society, many associate themselves with a god (note the little 'g'). Whether you're going to insist on a Christian hypnotist or not is your call. My point here is that what people say of themselves may not be what's real.

Remember what I said earlier: The only option in your area might be the non-Christian hypnotist. There are many fine non-Christian practitioners out there and I would be comfortable seeing them. The important thing is that you or your loved ones get the best care.

If you're concerned about a medical or dental procedure, you're not going to question the doctor or dentist's faith; you'll ask about the processes they use. Given that, I share areas of concern below that would give me pause.

AREAS OF CONCERN

This is an area where some of my non-Christian hypnotist friends might disagree with me. I believe the first area of concern for the Christian should be, "Past Life Regression".

As I noted earlier in Chapter 6, scripture says that we, "*Were appointed once to die*"[34] and I believe that past life regression is unhealthy to a walk with Jesus since it is contrary to God's word.

Others engage in, "Spirit Releasement" that deals with lost souls and the associated negative energies. I believe as Christians, we only have business seeking one spirit: the Holy Spirit.

I know some that work with "Dark Force Entities" dealing with evil spirits and demons that attach themselves to a person. Scripture tells us we should, "*Walk in the light*"[35]. Given that, we should avoid those who work in a dark realm.

That's not to say that I don't believe those dark entities exist; I do. If there was no evil in this world, I believe there would never have been sin. Yet, from the first few pages of the Bible, we see that humans quickly walked into trouble and sinned. And so, things changed.

It was because of our sinful nature that God sent His Son to die on our behalf on the cross. He won the battle against sin and death, and we now have been given the choice to pursue the light, and avoid the darkness that travels throughout this world.

Yes, there is evil in this world. Yes, there are evil spirits. But, we don't need to invite any interaction with them through curiosity or compromise.

PART 3

PUTTING IT
TO ACTION

13

Be A Part Of Change

If you're a Christian and you determine that a non-Christian practitioner is operating in areas contrary to your faith, please, don't condemn them in your heart or mind to hell. Pray for them: *"Lord, draw this person to a saving knowledge of you."* How long did it take to say that prayer? Three or four seconds? What did it cost you? Don't let pride or judgment interfere with drawing someone closer to God.

Hypnosis, when practiced within safe boundaries utilizes the physiology that God gave us and produces incredible positive changes. I envision a time when hypnosis will be accepted across the nation as it is in other parts of the world.

It wasn't that long ago that Chiropractic treatment was seen with skepticism. Today, those practitioners are seen as being part of a viable profession. With proper standards and training, I believe hypnotism can eventually be seen in the same light.

By educating the Christian population about the safe and effective realities of hypnosis, I'd like to see an emergence of Christian practitioners bringing healthy solutions to those in our congregations that need help.

Our churches are full of hurting people. While Christ came to save the lost, there are many that are saved…and yet still have doubts and fears about their eternal future.

It's wonderful when a person comes to a saving relationship with Jesus Christ. Yet, sometimes our worst tormentor is ourselves. The voice they live with is often their own repeating familiar messages from the devil. The lies forced upon them continue:

You are not smart enough…

You are not pretty or handsome enough…

You are not brave enough…

You are too old…

You are too fat…

You are too short…

You come from a bad family…

You are too poor…

You are not good enough…

When the destroyer keeps us focused on what we are not, he prevents us from becoming what we can be. People in our churches carry regrets for years that now seem to be lost time never regained. These regrets exacerbate the belief that they are stuck and will stay stuck, while fearing time will run out.

Left unchecked, fears can cause a person to spiral into a vortex of despair, and ultimately illness. A person living with regret for bad choices, or bad circumstances may feel condemned.

Perhaps the regret of a moment's choice that ended a relationship, broke a heart or caused some other damaging result, maintains just under the surface that they are unforgivable. All the while, such a person at the church will steel their emotions and façade to appear that all is well.

Yet, when in the quietness of themselves they hurt, feeling afraid to expose the thin shell that barely covers their pain. What they need is love, kindness, and acceptance while hiding their hurts.

Within our society and our churches are people that suffered abuses and heartaches, all the while growing proficient at pretending.

Those that carry the hurts from exclusion, exploitation or judgment either choose to be quiet and hold it in, or they move to another church or give up altogether and another soul is lost. The devil doesn't have to work hard. In fact, he can sleep late when there are those that judge and criticize, in essence, doing his work for him.

Our world is full of uncertainty. Look at the news on television, online or in print and you'll see the images of Matthew 24 coming to pass. Realistically, no Christian should be surprised because scripture tells us of Christ's return and we should understand the end times are coming.[36]

Granted, generations saw indications of those perilous times ahead. Has the world gotten harder or people cruel? I don't think so. Today, technology just makes it easier to cause damage, and then communicate the crimes and harshness quickly at a global level.

What I believe to be different is that generations ago, those in our churches were actually looking for Christ's return. Today, people are looking at the world from the perspective of how life revolves around them. Rather than, *"Watch and pray"*[37], people seek comfort in our churches and the world without thinking about or considering change, or how their actions impact others.

Any opinion counter to the comfortable is met with waving the *"I'm offended"* flag. If the target of the offended person reacts with judgment, condemnation or outright misbehavior, then that's seen as an acceptable response that now justifies the perpetrator's position in their mind.

What I've found is rather than actually research or think something through, argumentative positions are often nothing more than a parroted stance from some social network post by someone they don't even know.

WATCHING OUR WITNESS

I believe stolen social network opinions create a weak foundation for our witness. We cannot be what we are not. The fruit planted always produces that which comes from the seed. That being, the fruit that *we* produce is always from the seed within us. Our seed should always emulate the gifts of the Spirit. Otherwise, we create dissension and hurt. It's highly unlikely that we'll ever lead a person to Christ when our witness is critical or judgmental. I believe even our own prayers lose effectiveness when presented to God with a judging and unforgiving heart.

I understand some of the misperceptions of hypnosis within Christian circles. Yet, I also believe withholding the benefits of the work I'm doing to effect positive life change is harmful.

Christians are targeted at nearly every turn. Some are targeted physically, and others are attacked through slanderous words and opinion through courts and politics - all aimed at silencing any indication that represents Christ. Given the uncertainties of this world and the attempts to silence the Christian voice, shouldn't we seek to strengthen our churches – the congregations, the very people that represent our faith?

If there were a safe and effective way to help a person that endured years of abuse or misperception, isn't that a good thing? If a person can see themselves as what they are – a creation of God, a person without the need to walk through their days without judgment, then that's beneficial to their life.

If a person can gain their confidence while staying away from the areas of concern I noted earlier in this book, then they can see themselves as what they are – God's workmanship. Yes. That's a good thing.

As scripture tells us, "*As a man thinketh in his heart, so is he* ".[38] This is the first step to their turnaround. When they see themselves as successful, they are prepared for good things ahead. Look for the good and you'll find it. This is a basic foundation of goal setting. Set a goal and with each minor success, a sense of accomplishment grows, leading to greater successes.

14

Overcoming The Negative

In an earlier chapter, I talked about how the subconscious mind is protective in nature and yet forms our habits and perceptions. When a person is in a state of hypnosis, healthy suggestion to that part of the mind helps them free long-lasting fears, or the misperception that there's something wrong with them. Feeding a false belief prevents successful living.

There's no shortage of people waiting in line to tell us there's something wrong with us. Through hypnosis, a person can find the balance to persist amidst degrading or inflammatory talk thrown at them by people or their environment.

Hypnosis won't change the intentional narcissistic abuser – they are comfortable where they are, stealing power from others to point the attention at themselves. The challenge of narcissistic people causes years of hurts to people just trying to live their lives peacefully.

In recent years, there's been a steady increase of women that are reaching out to me for change in their lives because of the problems associated with abusers.

Hypnosis has shown to be a great help to them. Since the client is in control during hypnosis, they have to make a choice and decide that they have had enough and are ready to start moving forward in positive ways.

When victims choose to step up and be survivors, watching the transformation occur in front of me is an awesome experience. I work with women from abuse situations all the time. In many cases, the damage caused them from abusers originated decades earlier.

The effect of failed misperceptions about themselves leads them to a place of fear, worry and panic-like symptoms. They arrive tearful, and leave confident, focused and cheerful with a plan to live a healthy, happy life. After seeing this frequent life transformation, no one can convince me that hypnosis is bad.

WHERE CREDIT IS DUE

Even though I incorporate a series of processes that help my clients, I don't take credit for the results. First, I give credit where it is due: to God. Before every session, before any client even arrives, I'm in the chair praying for them…Christian or not. I pray the Holy Spirit fill the entire building, parking lot, every room, corner or crevice. I pray that every word, thought or attitude is God-honoring and anything with an evil intent will stay away.

I then pray for each client that they will receive the life-changing benefit as God would have them receive. Let them feel safe, secure, comfortable and be expectant of good change in their lives.

Then, I pray that God will lead me to see, hear, think, feel, say, notice, or do as He would lead for my client's best benefit.

There have been quite a few times when I'll start a session with a plan in mind, then felt led to shift in another direction. Each time, those shifts brought out issues and incredible changes occurred that I didn't see coming.

I've been saying this prayer since day one. I believe it is God-honoring and an integral reason why certain clients contact me from all over the U.S. I believe God points the right people toward me at a time when they are ready.

While it's true that I have processes that help them release their old baggage, I'm just taking them on a path they need to travel, but they wouldn't have thought to go there without my help. It is the client that steps up and works through it with me. When they choose to allow the change to happen, they realize they are part of the solution, and they have the ability to overcome obstacles. The blessing I receive is watching it happen.

LIVING AMIDST HARD MESSAGES

As Christians we are given hard messages in the bible. Love your neighbor. What if they live a life that is counter to everything that you stand for? What if your neighbor seems normal enough and yet, somehow annoys you? Who is your neighbor?

They could be the person at work that criticizes or gossips or the person at the grocery store that is rude to you. Your neighbor could be a person you don't even know or expect to walk into your life. They (like you and I) might need kindness. How will we respond while we are focusing on our own issues?

Scripture tells us to love our enemy. Wouldn't it be easier if we could call down lightning and blast them? How many times have we heard, "*Love the sinner and hate the sin*"? How many times do we fail at that each day? Hypnosis is a great life balancer to help our lives and be there for the "neighbor" around us.

As I noted earlier in Chapter 13, scripture tells us that a man is according to what he thinks.   We attract what we think about. We attract kindness by being kind. We attract good, loving people by being one. We attract a simple smile that can completely change your day by sharing a smile with others.

In like fashion, in hypnosis as you focus upon positive suggestions, you in turn become the benefactor of the results by attracting them. You can control your 0 to 60 mile per hour reactions, build your confidence, calm your worries, be kind, loving and happy with your life, simply by allowing positive suggestion to reach your subconscious mind in hypnosis.

I didn't make this up – God planned it this way. We reap what we sow. I like a saying that Dr. Charles Stanley says: "You reap what you sow, more than you sow, later than you sow."[39] I see this all the time with my hypnosis clients.

They often arrive uncertain of me, hypnosis and themselves. They lack confidence and live in a state of free-floating fear. They tell me they feel like complete failures because they are overcome by negative habits. The life they live is the result of an emotional shell that prevents them from breaking out to enjoy a healthy, happy life. Instead, they are held within a cocoon of emotional misbeliefs and weakness.

In this world, the weak are targeted and seen as easy marks by bullies and other weak minded people. With each verbal, physical, psychological, emotional or sexual hit they take, they drop further into a vortex with no apparent escape. The cocoon they've built around them gets harder and harder. Even the most kind-hearted person can become angry, bitter and untrusting. If that person portrays (or sows) the life they believe is one of failure, what life will they reap in return?

In an effort to ease the pain, loneliness or shame from living a life that's totally counter to the life they want, they bury their feelings in negative habits. People begin to over-eat, drink, smoke, engage in drug use or some other destructive behavior to shield the emotional reality of the life they are living. The habits don't resolve the underlying issues. In fact, they amplify the negative beliefs they are feeling. As they succeed in failing, they drop further into that vortex of un-living.

Many times, those negative self-beliefs are amplified by the bullies I noted earlier, and many times they are coworkers or family. The victim of this behavior often finds themselves walking on eggshells from the abusive behaviors by others.

Their internal reality of living a life held back creates a fear of trying since the belief is that all will fail anyway. This can be a dangerous place because the value of life for some degrades into the potential for more self-harm.

I see this all the time since my clients primarily come from extremely abusive situations. We work through their fears, uncertainties of me, hypnosis and themselves. Then, a shift begins where they gain a new sense of confidence and self-control. Their prior negative self-perception is replaced with a healthier self-loving view and life begins moving in a good direction. As we incorporate stress management as part of their daily regimen for self-care, I've seen clients begin to physically change.

15

Physical Change

I remember the first time I observed a near-instant physical change. An out of town psychologist sent me a referral for a young woman that lived in a state of fear most of her life. Her life was an unhealthy balance of frequent panic attacks and medications.

We can try to convince ourselves that internal fears will go away, but that's as useful as trying to skateboard uphill. Unchecked, fears get bigger and the effect on our lives gets stronger. It's like a small piece of clay that we put into our pocket with each challenging moment. With each unwelcome visit by fear, we place another little piece of clay into our pocket. Over time, those little bits of clay merge into a larger weight that we carry around with us each day. Eventually, we are held back and held down, hostage to our own feelings.

This young woman struggled with fears most of her life. She chose to use willpower and push through each time she felt that familiar uneasiness that often grew into a sense of panic.

To her credit, she did pursue help through licensed therapists and stayed medicated every day for years. The prescription drugs numbed her emotions and ability to find the balance to maintain a job, a boyfriend and live a happy life.

She trained and held a successful position in a salon that assisted women with makeup and beauty choices. The job seemed a good fit for her as she is proficient, has a good eye and personality for that work.

Even with a good job and a supporting boyfriend, fear if unaddressed will continue to grow larger. She found herself waking each morning in a near-panic state and struggled to even leave her home. Her doctors found that dosing changes of her medications were becoming an exploratory case of hit and miss. They suggested that she see me.

As we began to address the historical and subsequent feelings while in hypnosis, her subconscious mind began to get it. Her self-perception was changing and she allowed herself to realize she's not to blame for events that occurred as a small child.

Even things that appear insignificant as an adult, were in fact, planting the seeds for her later feelings and beliefs. Those fearful events grew within her and became a large hurdle in the way of the life she hoped to live. Given this new sense of clarity, she made a choice to see things clearer and respond in healthy ways that support her.

With the realization that her past does not control her future, she allowed herself to live confidently and accept opportunities to live contently. The stress dissipated and she found it easier to breathe. Previously, her jaw, neck, shoulders, and chest were tight, and she was constantly breathing fast shallow breaths.

After our last session, I noticed her skin looked healthier, her eyes were brighter, she stood taller, smiled and she spoke confidently. Was this hypnosis that did this? Every thought creates a chemical reaction in our bodies. We used hypnosis to help her overcome the false belief that her life was tainted because of misbehaviors by others. Through that work, she allowed herself to be freed of a bad history.

Hypnosis brought change to her self-perceptions and beliefs. The physical result was from a simple release of stress. Her face and body no longer had the tightened muscles and capillaries in her skin. Basically, healthy blood flow now nourished her when the stress was gone.

As an observer, it was an amazing sight. After reaching out to more experienced practitioners, many told me of the same observations in their clients. One very well-respected medically-trained hypnotist told me how a large part of her practice is using hypnosis for ongoing health and beauty care. Over the succeeding years, I've been given this incredible gift of watching my client's life and physical appearance change right in front of me.

16

Emotional Triggers

In an earlier chapter, we talked about the formation of habits. This chapter looks closer at the behaviors that result from negative triggers. I've watched clients arrive for years with a variety of habits and the underlying causes are as varied and unique as there are fingerprints in the world. As humans, we are each unique individuals and we respond with different emotions to events and our environment in ways that are personal to us.

There is no defined formula that says, "If a person has "x" habit, then "a", "b", or "c" must have happened. Therefore, we'll pull out a specific recipe to resolve the issue. Likewise, two people with the same background could experience a similar event and their subsequent responses could be inversely proportional to each other.

One female client came to see me because she struggled to overcome her weight management challenges. During the sessions, we found that as a young child, she was left alone by her mother. From the perspective of a young child, she was afraid something happened to her mother. That led to: *I'm alone. What will happen to me?*

The spinning of logic and scenarios from the mind of a child made her fearful whenever she was alone. Throughout her life, she linked, "Being alone" with feeling afraid. In an attempt to minimize the fear, she resorted to eating comfort foods. This became problematic during her teenage years when she was looking for acceptance from her peers.

Being one of the heavier girls, she was often excluded from group activities. That sense of isolation amplified the "alone" feeling and subsequent fear that she'll always be living a solitary life. In an attempt to distract her feelings of loneliness, she ate and continued to cover her feelings with comfort foods.

SIMILAR EVENTS PROCESS DIFFERENTLY

Another woman came to see me because she struggled with confidence most of her life and often failed at developing healthy relationships. Just like the previous scenario, as a child, she was often left alone. She loved her Mommy and Daddy dearly, yet they rarely spent much time with her. In the mind of a young child, she perceived this as being unwanted and unloved.

The sadness continued into her young adult years with the perception that there must be something wrong with her. This false perception of herself made her feel unworthy of a loving relationship.

As she grew older and wanted acceptance and inclusion of her peer network, she often tried too hard and would cling to her friends so much that her behavior often caused them to flee from her. Once again, the result of her attempts to be happy and included left her with disappointment and feeling incapable and unworthy.

Over time, she found herself accepting any guy that would show her attention. Even her female counterparts became an easy mark for her unintended grip for their attention. As her behavior continued to isolate herself, she reached a point where she accepted the belief that she would live an unhappy, solitary life. She then covered her feelings with smoking, over-eating, marijuana and designer drugs.

While conducting a regression, we found that her parents did love her. During her early years, the family struggled financially and both parents worked long hours and various schedules. The parents tried to shield her from the worry they were enduring, many times leaving her alone.

As an adult able to look back and see the situation, she gained a new perspective. There was nothing wrong with her, then or now and she currently is and was loved by her parents.

Armed with this new awareness that she really can live a healthy life and make good relationship choices. She has since taken control of her habits and her social life is one of inclusion rather than exclusion.

This situation mirrors many of the clients that come to see me. It's a sad situation when you see the decades of lost love and living held back because of early misperceptions.

I wonder how many tears are shed in our world, our workplaces, our homes, and our churches because of misunderstanding, pride, fear or ego that keeps building walls, separating us from the potential goodness and love we could have lived.

17

An Orchard & Our Beliefs

As a young boy, I remember living in a trailer park in San Diego, California. Back in those days, we didn't have much, so as kids we made the best of our time outside. Nearby were some hills to climb and dried grass to slide down on pieces of found cardboard. Further up the hill and to the left was a large avocado orchard.

Under that thick canopy of trees, the shade gave coolness on even the hottest days. My friends and I would run through the knee-high piles of leaves and play. All around us were dark green avocados growing on each of the trees. I estimate there were thousands, or maybe even tens of thousands in that huge orchard.

Back then, I never tried an avocado and even though they were plentiful all around me, for some reason, I believed I didn't like them. Was that determination based upon some experiential fact? No. Was it based upon some warning that they are bad for me? No. Was it based upon something that someone said to me or some thought that came to mind? I don't know. I just decided they were bad. That was the belief I formed from somewhere.

This is how many feel about hypnosis today. They have no actual experience to draw from and in spite of mountains of scientific and medical research attributing positive outcomes from hypnosis some determine it as bad. This mindset often originates within religious circles, not always, but a lot. Some counter to hypnosis, or other self-proclaimed experts declare with zealous intention that hypnosis is bad. That claim is often followed by an assertion that a hypnotist is of the devil.

The same people that declare hypnosis as a bad thing, and associate it with worshiping evil, have never experienced hypnosis other than the natural states they transition in and out of each day. These same people have not researched to form an intelligent position. I've had some tell me that I have no business reading science to support hypnosis. According to them, I should only read the bible.

Here's where I stand on that: I believe God created everything. Why? Because His word says so in Genesis. That means He also created science. It is a supportive process to validate what we already know about the biblical truths of history.

Yet, there's also a large movement in our world today that seeks to invalidate the truth of God's existence, His Son who died for us, and His rising again to conquer sin. As a Christian, I am happy when archeological digs or other science support the truths we already know from the bible. Yet, God doesn't need science to help Him out or prove He exists; He does exist. Science helps us to grab onto those truths and know Him better.

For those few that suggest that we should avoid science to show healthy outcomes with hypnosis, we cannot then, choose science to validate an argument of God. We just don't get to have it both ways.

I've also had people tell me they don't believe in hypnosis, then tell me hypnosis is used for past life regression. Wait a minute. Let's deconstruct this. If a person does not believe in hypnosis, how can they say something that doesn't exist is used to justify a past life?

And, if as a Christian, a person believes in God's word that says, *"We are appointed once to die"*[40], how can they then say that hypnosis is used for something they don't believe in? Do you see how messy this argument gets?

Perhaps we should focus on less argument and more on Christ-like living. Even that statement will mess some people up because we are in a world where people will call themselves a "Spiritual" person. What does that mean?

Being spiritual can mean just about anything to justify a particular practice or belief. I believe that Christ is the ONE way to heaven. Why? Because God said so. Others will say, "Many roads lead there", and yet, we each consider ourselves spiritual.

To be honest, given the disparity of practitioners that engage in areas that I believe are spiritually unhealthy as I noted in Chapter 12, how is a person without experience to know better?

As a Christian, I believe scripture should lay the foundation for our beliefs and behaviors when it is addressed. Yet, in the case of scripture, hypnosis is not addressed. Show me a chapter or verse that says hypnosis is bad or that it honors the devil. It's not there.

Let's not get our vernacular confused. Those who counter with the argument that hypnosis is bad without tangible scientific knowledge automatically equates the hypnotist as bad. I said near the beginning of this book, that I am a Christian first and a hypnotist second. As a Christian that practices hypnosis to help people regain their life after abuse or emotional trauma, does that make me bad? I don't believe that.

Earlier, I discussed concerns that a Christian might consider when searching out the right hypnotist to help them fully benefit in a safe way. On these points, this might be the only place where some in religious circles agree with me for a moment.

This is also a place where some respected friends and peers within the hypnotism profession might cringe as it seems to pull away from the marketing value of our profession. I believe stating my position from a Christian perspective is more important than mincing words.

There are many great non-Christian hypnotists that help people in remarkable ways each day and I would refer to them with ease. Hypnotism is a safe, healthy, drug-free process, bringing a positive life-changing result.

18

Final Thoughts

Throughout this book, I've discussed what hypnosis is and what it is not. We've seen it is a natural process that we all experience each day. When applied to a client with a sense of focused concentration, their fears and worries, misperceptions, and unhealthy stress responses can return to a place where the individual can gain an entirely new insight about themselves. There was a time when I didn't even believe that hypnosis was a viable resource for regaining a life after years of misperceived beliefs, or abusive events. To me, hypnosis was no different than any other stage performance, solely for entertainment purposes.

Very early in this text, I asked you as the reader to look at the issue of hypnosis objectively as a potential contributor to your life. We have all had road bumps in our lives that sometimes looked like fear, worry, anger or self-confidence issues. It becomes very easy to play the comparison game with others living their lives as they compare themselves with the world around them.

False beliefs that form during a comparative existence creates an unhealthy threshold that determines the line between happy living, or a sad struggle. The emotional triggers that people carry can literally stunt a person's potential future if allowed to take root.

Perhaps in your own situation, you wonder what your life could be like if things were different. So many things are impacted by underlying emotional triggers and beliefs. They impact our relationships, our self-view, or willingness to accomplish things, rather than procrastinate and push it off until the right time arrives. The right time will never arrive until we decide that enough is enough and we seek to be a part of the process.

Hypnosis is a participation sport. You might remember early in this book that I said you are in control when hypnotized. This is especially true for the work I do. I address emotional triggers that need to be undone so you can move forward and live without dragging the old past around with you. That's done in hypnosis by taking an honest view of the way things really are and pointing the subconscious mind in the right directions.

When interacting with the subconscious mind at a deeper, emotional level, new connections and beliefs are formed to get you to the life you want to live. In my very early days, I didn't fully understand the importance of screening clients that are willing to do the work from those that just want to sit in the chair, close their eyes and say, "*Okay, fix me*". There's great value in being an active participant in the process because you get to see the change that was created with you in the driver's seat.

My purpose is to empower people in healthy ways. Looking back in Chapter Eight, we discussed how these processes can help a person, strengthen a marriage, and empower children. You can create generations of new successes just by being part of that change.

SUCCESS WITH HYPNOSIS

I've had the privilege of watching lives change in front of me. Both men and women were freed from hidden fears they carried while pretending that all is well. Within their work environment, it was always safer to avoid the stigma of a person *"with a problem"*. All the while, dealing with the ensuing stress upon their minds and bodies.

Other clients arrived because of their compulsion to smoke, chew tobacco, over-eat, and many other unhealthy habits. By addressing the hidden emotional reasons below the surface, they quickly saw the change in their lives.

One woman from years ago still stands out vividly in my mind. As a professional in city government, this woman smoked heavily for over two decades. Yet, she somehow hid from her co-workers the fact that she was ever a smoker.

During her sessions, I told her that she is *"In control over things she allows into her body and from that moment forward, she will find better use of the expense of tobacco and start applying it to a better future."*

A few weeks later, I checked on her to see how she was doing. She told me that she quit smoking completely and any time that she thought of cigarettes, rather than smoke, she went online and transferred the cost of cigarettes into a savings account. I didn't come up with that idea – she did. That's how her subconscious mind took the positive suggestion and applied it proactively to her life.

In another scenario, a man showed up in the office with a huge beard, unkempt hair, dirty clothes, and in need of a serious bath. My initial thoughts weren't my proudest moments. Fortunately, I checked myself and realized that standing before me was a man that lacked financial means. In his eyes, I could see he needed help. When he got into the chair, I could see he had significant discomfort.

I asked him how he was feeling. Was he under the care of a doctor and if so, would he like to postpone the visit? He told me he only sees his doctor to keep a prescription going. Then, he told me a story that you just can't make up about an ex-wife. Decades earlier, she tried to run him over with an old car. That's where his injuries came from. Then, he excitedly told me, *"I'm good. This is a good day because today I'm going to quit smoking!"*

This man smoked for 30-years and was beginning to feel a bit winded. He would work all day long and refrain from taking any medication to stay on the job. At home, his current wife was bed-bound for years from other serious medical conditions. He described how he'd go without medication all day, and then come home to have dinner with his wife. Around 7:00 pm each night, he'd take his meds and go to bed, then do it all over again the next day.

This was a learning moment for me. I wasn't proud of my own initial perception when he arrived. Now, I was impressed with this man – he was a stand-up guy that took true responsibility to heart. I felt (and still do feel) privileged to help this man.

We had our session and then agreed to a follow-up two days

later. On that day, in walked a man that was clean-shaven, bathed, wearing a clean shirt, standing taller with a smile on his face. I almost didn't recognize him. He told me that two-days earlier, he went home and had dinner with his wife. Then, rather than take his meds, he went out to the shop behind the house and began building hope chests for his grandkids.

According to him, he had not been out to his wood shop in a few years. He didn't smoke or want to since. I still felt like a new hypnotist back then and this was an important personal refining moment for me.

As I described in Chapter 14, as a Christian hypnotist, I pray for each client before they arrive. Back then, I was still figuring out my practice and the approaches I would use to help. I was praying, *"Lord, bring me those people that you want me to help."*

God always answers prayer, sometimes on a schedule inconvenient to us, but He always answers – sometimes through action and at other times through silence. In these early days, this was one of many prayers He answered.

I believe that God began bringing me a type of client I didn't expect: Women that carried the effects of decades of serious abuse – physical, psychological, emotional and sexual. These clients began arriving from all over the country. The remarkable thing is that I didn't advertise other than a website. I believe God was pointing the right people to me at a time when they were ready to take personal action.

If anything will make a practitioner pray, it's these types of clients. The stories I hear can take the breath out of you at times. If it weren't for the prayer covering beforehand, I don't know if I could do this work.

I also found very quickly that abuse is not limited to a certain level of the social strata. I've had medical professionals, government and corporate executives, celebrities, a movie producer, business owners, military veterans, law enforcement, first responders, housewives, non-profit coordinators, senior citizens, and women that escaped the dark world of human trafficking. My clients represent racial, cultural and a variety of religious and non-religious backgrounds.

Abuse does not discriminate.

I remember an early abuse case with a woman. As the session began and we dealt with the emotional lies that she was forced to carry for nearly three decades. The tears began pouring out. As her makeup was drenched, I didn't want her to emerge from her session feeling embarrassed for looking like an emotional raccoon with dripping makeup. I began gently catching the tears with a soft tissue as we worked through the issues.

I've watched the releasing of decades of emotional weight during those processes, and the emergence of a new, confident and happy person. When combining the deep subconscious level with emotions, the results can give the client freedom.

Recently, given global divisiveness and uncertainty over crime, family, personal health and relationship concerns, finances, politics, terrorism or war, I'm seeing a new shift in the client's that arrive. Many of them share much of the same abuse scenarios.

Yet, their reason for choosing to see me now is the stress reaction to the world around them. They typically describe a feeling of being overwhelmed that leaves them in a state of being frozen in fear and uncertainty.

Through hypnosis, we begin stress work and confidence building. Like the abuse clients, we deal with the emotional triggers and collectively begin to see quick refreshment of the uncomfortable conditions they carried.

One of these clients reached out to me after being promoted to a management position. He described being overwhelmed at the thought of operating a business and keeping things running well. We began our sessions and he quickly began to realize that he really does have the knowledge, skills, and abilities to be proficient.

After our last session, he described releasing two problem employees, hiring new ones and restructuring the business. The fears that once existed are gone. Now he sees the positive changes in his life and those around him.

These are just a few examples of life restoration that came as a result of incorporating hypnosis to build and strengthen the client. There are many sad and hurting people in our churches, workplaces, and public spaces.

In a recent church service, members had the opportunity to place the names of people they feel they need to forgive on a card. Each card was anonymous and intended to be prayed over by the Elders. Others noted areas where they feel they need God's intervention of personal challenges or wanted to confess forgiveness. Granted, God is here for us in our lives in any place and at any time and nothing is too big for Him.[41] Yet, this process helped to make it a tangible experience.

According to the Pastor, almost 80 people had someone they

wanted to forgive. Realistically, forgiveness is a strong foundation of our faith. God sent His Son to die on the cross for us. Three days later, He rose from the dead to conquer sin and death. Yet, our ability to receive salvation begins with asking forgiveness for our sin and accepting Him as our Lord and Savior.

The Pastor described pulling the anonymous cards out to pray for them. Here are just a few of the many that he read:

Lord help me with my jealousy, my hurts, my marriage, my depression, my loneliness, to accept myself as you do, my fear, my anxiety, my anger, not to judge people, not to give up on myself, and my stress.

These are real issues by real people just trying to live their lives. We don't know the basis of their challenges. Maybe they are alone, dealing with a family, health issue or work environment. Maybe they feel as though no one is there for them. We don't know, but God does. Of the twelve challenges noted above, if you're alive, then you (just like me) have felt at least ten of these at some point in life. Given what you now know at the end of this book, hypnosis with a qualified practitioner might be a viable option to help you or someone you love.

When someone carries emotional hurts and false beliefs that they are broken in some way, it impacts those around them. Hypnosis, being a safe a natural process cannot change the past, but it can help a person create healthy strategies to use the knowledge of the past to move forward confidently.

Years ago, if someone were to tell me I would be a hypnotist, I would have thought they were crazy. Now, years later, I've seen the life-restorative power of hypnosis through many clients. If there are things in your life that seem to keep you stuck, the choice to allow change begins with you. It's my prayer that you will consider this natural, life-changing process to move into a life that you were created for.

Though I once had doubts about hypnosis, I've seen many people regain their life over these last few years. Today, I'm convinced hypnosis offers you a renewing of your mind.

MAKING A CHOICE THAT MATTERS

If you've been working your way through life and still wondering how your efforts will play out, let me tell you...God sent His Son to suffer and die on the cross for our sins. He rose three days later and conquered death to give you and me the opportunity for an eternal future, one that is greater than anything we can possibly imagine.

Romans 10:9 says, *"If you declare with your mouth, "Jesus is Lord," and believe in your heart that God raised him from the dead, you will be saved."*

All we need to do is ask Him to forgive us of our sins and become the Lord of our life. I pray the seeds planted in this book grow bountifully in your life to seek and receive the eternal blessings awaiting you. Realistically, it is the easiest and most beneficial decision you can ever make in this life.

Blessings,

Anthony M. Davis

"Here I am! I stand at the door and knock. If anyone hears my voice and opens the door, I will come in and eat with that person, and they with me."[42]

ABOUT THE AUTHOR

Anthony M. Davis is the Director of the Center for Personal Leadership and Development in Charlottesville, Virginia. He is a Board Certified Hypnotist, and a Certified Leadership, Success and Stress Coach.

Mr. Davis served in two military services. Beginning with the United States Navy, he served as a Helicopter Rescue Aircrew member. Later, he rejoined the military and retired from the United States Coast Guard. Shortly after 9/11, he was selected as the Intelligence Chief with the USCG Marine Safety Office, Mobile, AL. Upon retiring from the service, he once again served the Coast Guard as a Civilian Federal Maritime Investigator. He is the author of, *"Terrorism and the Maritime Transportation System"*.

In 2003, He was selected as the Federal Employee of the Year for Civil Law Enforcement, and the prestigious International Association of Law Enforcement Intelligence Analyst's (IALEIA) 2004 Professional Service award.

As a Board Certified Hypnotist, Mr. Davis serves clients nationwide and he is recognized nationally for his successes with victims of abuse & emotional distress to regain confident & contented living in a short period of time.

He is a successful Leadership, Success & Stress Coach, helping business professionals, transitioning military & goal-oriented individuals achieve new levels of success.

BIBLIOGRAPHY

1 John 1:7. In *New International Version Bible.*

2 Timothy 2:15, In *King James Version Bible.*

Acts Chapter 9. In *New International Version Bible.*

Banyan, Calvin. D., Kein, Gerald F. (2001). *Hypnosis and Hypnotherapy: Basic to Advanced Techniques and Procedures for the Professional.* Banyan Hypnosis Center.

Banyan, Calvin. D. (2004). *Hypnosis and Hypnotherapy Patter Scripts and Techniques.* Banyan Publishing, Inc.

Banyan Hypnosis Center. (2007). 7th PATH ®.

Banyan Hypnosis Center. (2007). 5 PATH ®.

Baring-Gould, S. (1865). Onward, Christian Soldiers [Music by Arthur Sullivan].

Davis, A. M. . *Welcome Page.* Retrieved from Healing Hypnosis: http://www.healing-hypnosis.org

Ephesians 6:11. In *New International Version Bible.*

Ephesians 6:13. In *New International Version Bible.*

Ephesians 6:14. In *New International Version Bible.*

Ephesians 6:17. In *New International Version Bible.*

Eslinger, M. Ron. (2013). *Hypnosis: Putting the Imagination to Work.* Healthy Visions.

Google. Retrieved from http://www.google.com

Hebrews 9:27, In *King James Version Bible.*

Isaiah 64:6. In *New International Version Bible.*

James 1:2. In *New American Standard Bible (NASB).*

Jeremiah 31:34. In *King James Version Bible.*

Jonah 1:1-17. In *New International Version Bible.*

Katayama, H., Gianotti, L. R., Isotani, T., Faber, P. L., Sasada, K., Kinoshita, T., & Lehmann, D. (2007). Classes of multichannel EEG microstates in light and deep hypnotic conditions. *Brain Topography, 20*(1), 7-14.

Matthew 26:41. In *New International Version Bible.*

Matthew Chapter 24. In *New International Version Bible.*

National Guild of Hypnotists. (2017). *Code of Ethics.* Retrieved from https://ngh.net/wp-content/uploads/2010/12/CodeEthicsStandards.pdf

National Guild of Hypnotists. *http://www.ngh.net.*

Parkinson, Anna. (2014). *Change Your Mind, Heal Your Body.* Watkins Publishing.

Peale, Norman. V. (1952). *The power of positive thinking.* New York, NY: Prentice-Hall.

Pew Forum. *Religious Landscape Study.* Retrieved from http://www.pewforum.org/religious-landscape-study

Proverbs 22:6. In *King James Version Bible.*

Proverbs 23:7. In *King James Version Bible.*

Psalm 1:7. In *King James Version Bible* .

Psalm 17:22. In *New International Version Bible.*

Psalm 91:11. In *New International Version Bible.*

Revelation 3:20, In *New International Version Bible.*

Romans 5:8. In *New International Version Bible.*

Romans 8:28, In *New International Version Bible.*

Stanley, Charles. F. (2014, July 16). *Life Principle 6: The Principle of Sowing and Reaping.* Retrieved from In Touch Ministries: https://www.intouch.org/read/life-principle-6-the-principle-of-sowing-and-reaping

INDEX

THANK YOU FOR READING

Thank you for reading my book. For years now, people arrive carrying the effects of stress, panic modes and worry, afraid that their future lacks any goodness. The pain, stress, fears and tormenting memories from abuse situations were all they could see on their horizon.

The people seeking help are just like you and me. They once had hopes, dreams, and ambitions for the future but were stuck. After years of talk therapy or medication, their non-results left them feeling even more desolate in their sad desert.

After reading this text, you now have a clearer view of hypnosis as a safe process intended to help overcome false beliefs that held them back for years. If you had a friend or loved one stuck in their life. Wouldn't you like to see them live a happier and fulfilled life? I think you would.

I understand that we may not agree on every point in this book. Yet, this book is written to offer solutions to hurting in this world. I think we agree there is too much hurt in the world. This Large Print edition was also written to help those struggling while also visually challenged.

One way to help get the message out about this important book is to spread the word and post a review on the Amazon Book page associated with this text. **You can be a part of the solution** to help people. Please…If you like this book or gained new insights in some way, please leave a kind book review and help. Thank you.

ENDNOTES

1 Katayama, H., Gianotti, L. R. R., Isotani, T., Faber, P. L., Sasada, K., Kinoshita, T., & Lehmann, D. (2007). Classes of multichannel EEG microstates in light and deep hypnotic conditions. Brain Topography, 20(1), 7-14. http://dx.doi.org/10.1007/s10548-007-0024-3

2 Peale, Norman Vincent. 1952. The Power of Positive Thinking. New York: Prentice-Hall.

3 The Banyan Hypnosis Center. (2007). 7th PATH ®.

4 2 Timothy 2:15, King James Version Bible

5 National Guild of Hypnotists, http://www.ngh.net

6 The Banyan Hypnosis Center, 5-PATH®

7 Psalm 17:22, New International Version Bible.

8 Banyan, Calvin D., Hypnosis and Hypnotherapy Patter Scripts and Techniques, 2004. Banyan Publishing, Inc.

9 Banyan, Calvin D., Kein, Gerald F. , Hypnosis and Hypnotherapy: Basic to Advanced Techniques and Procedures for the Professional, 2001. Banyan Hypnosis Center.

10 Parkinson, Anna, *Change Your Mind, Heal Your Body*, 2014. Watkins Publishing.

11 Eslinger, M. Ron, *Hypnosis: Putting the Imagination to Work*, 2013. Healthy Visions.

12 Hebrews 9:27, King James Version Bible.

13 http://www.google.com, Google, Search Engine.

[14]Proverbs 22:6, King James Version Bible.

[15]Onward, Christian Soldiers, (1865). Lyrics: Baring-Gould, Sabine; Music: Sullivan, Arthur.

[16]Jonah 1:1-17, New International Version Bible.

[17]Isaiah 64:6, New International Version Bible.

[18]James 1:2, New American Standard Bible.

[19]Romans 5:8, New International Version Bible.

[20]Ephesians 6:11, New International Version Bible.

[21]Ephesians 6:13, New International Version Bible.

[22]Ephesians 6:14, New International Version Bible.

[23]Ibid.

[24]Ephesians 6:17, New International Version Bible.

[25]Psalm 91:11, New International Version Bible.

[26] Ibid.

[27]Proverbs 1:7, King James Version Bible.

[28]Jeremiah 31:34, King James Version Bible.

[29]Acts Chapter 9: New International Version Bible.

[30]Code of Ethics, National Guild of Hypnotists. 2017. Website: https://ngh.net/wp-content/uploads/2010/12/CodeEthicsStandards.pdf

[31]Ibid.

[32]Davis, A. M. *Welcome Page.* Retrieved from Healing Hypnosis: http://www.healing-hypnosis.org

[33]http://www.pewforum.org/religious-landscape-study

[34]Ibid.

[35]1 John 1:7, New International Version Bible.

[36]Matthew Chapter 24, New International Version Bible.

[37]Matthew 26:41, New International Version Bible.

[38]Proverbs 23:7, King James Version Bible.

[39]Stanley, Charles. F. (2014, July 16). *Life Principle 6: The Principle of Sowing and Reaping*. Retrieved from In Touch Ministries: https://www.intouch.org/read/life-principle-6-the-principle-of-sowing-and-reaping

[40]Ibid.

[41] Romans 8:28, New International Version Bible.

[42] Revelation 3:20, New International Version Bible.

www.ingramcontent.com/pod-product-compliance
Lightning Source LLC
Chambersburg PA
CBHW082358270326
41935CB00013B/1666